Soweto
16 June 1976

Personal Accounts of the Uprising

Compiled by Elsabé Brink, Gandhi Malungane,
Steve Lebelo, Dumisani Ntshangase and Sue Krige

Kwela Books

This book was originally published in 2001 to commemorate the 25th anniversary of 16 June 1976. The first edition was titled *Recollected 25 years later: Soweto, 16 June 1976 – It all started with a dog . . .*

Copyright text © 2001 Elsabé Brink et al

Published by Kwela Books,
An imprint of NB Publishers
40 Heerengracht, Cape Town, South Africa
PO Box 6525, Roggebaai, 8012, South Africa
www.kwela.com

Cover photograph by Mike Mzileni © BAHA Photo
Cover design by Nita Nagar, Oryx Media Productions
Typography by Nazli Jacobs
Set in Melior
Printed and bound by Interpak Books, Pietermaritzburg, South Africa
First edition, first impression 2001
Second edition, first impression 2006
Fourth impression 2012

ISBN: 978-0-7957-0232-7

First print-on-demand edition, first impression 2012
Fifth impression 2017
Printed and bound by CTP Printers, Cape Town
Tygerberg Business Park, Parow Industria, Cape Town

Dedication

This book is dedicated to Abe Lebelo
and all the young people who died in 1976
whose names we do not know.
It is dedicated to those who survived.
And to those who agreed to speak to us
about their experiences.

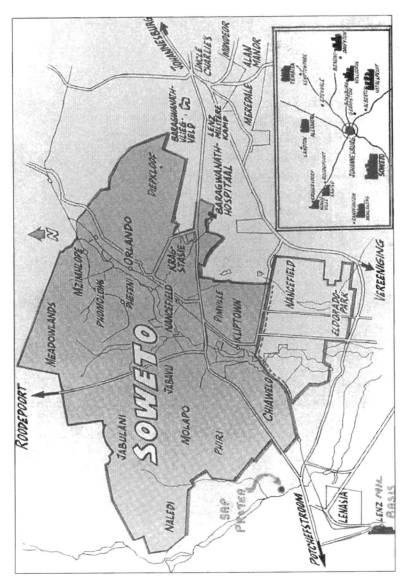

On 20 June 1976 the Sunday newspaper *Rapport* carried this map to identify for its mainly white readers the townships which made up Soweto at the time: Naledi in the far west, Meadowlands in the north, Chiawelo in the south, and Diepkloof in the east, the one closest to Johannesburg. Major freeways such as the N1 around Johannesburg and Soweto did not yet exist and Old Potchefstroom Road ran through Soweto to Potchefstroom and Klerksdorp in the western Transvaal. At Uncle Charlie's Roadhouse, the most important junction south of Johannesburg, the roads from Potchefstroom, Vereeniging and Johannesburg's southern suburbs converged. Courtesy *Rapport*

Contents

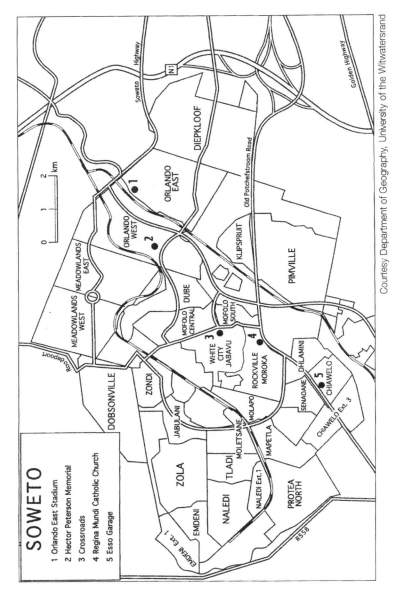

SOWETO

1 Orlando East Stadium
2 Hector Peterson Memorial
3 Crossroads
4 Regina Mundi Catholic Church
5 Esso Garage

2001: Soweto as it is today includes townships which were developed after 1976, such as Protea in the south-west. In addition, extensions were added to among others Diepkloof, Pimville and Dobsonville which were newly established in the early 1970s.

The Soweto uprising

ON THE MORNING OF WEDNESDAY, 16 June 1976, 20 000 Soweto school-children marched to protest against a decree by the South African government's Department of Bantu Education that Afrikaans had to be used as one of the languages of instruction in secondary schools. Within hours the initial peaceful and high-spirited march had sparked off a violent confrontation with the police which in little more than a week claimed at least 176 lives.

Apparently no order from the police to the marchers to disperse was heard, and no warning shots were fired. A thirteen-year-old Orlando West schoolboy called Hector Peterson was the first child to be shot. Several other youngsters were also killed. Complete chaos broke loose. Police vehicles were stoned and set on fire; police dogs were unleashed upon the students. Vehicles belonging to the West Rand Bantu Affairs Administration Board, which administered Soweto on behalf of the Department of Bantu Administration and Development, were burnt, and nearly all its offices in Soweto destroyed. Commercial vehicles and delivery vans of white-owned businesses were also set on fire. Beer halls and liquor stores were burnt and looted. Two white officials of the West Rand Administration Board were beaten to death.

The government closed the schools and sent its anti-riot unit into Soweto. The army was placed on the alert, and troops were mustered outside Soweto. In little more than 24 hours the violence and shooting had spread all over the 28 townships, covering 72 square kilometres, which constitute the Soweto complex. Within a few days 143 vehicles (among them 50 belonging to the police) and 139 buildings (including 33 Bantu Administration and Development buildings) had been damaged by fire or burnt out.

The violence spread from Soweto to other townships on the Reef and around Pretoria, and further afield. Within two months of 16 June, at least 80 black communities all over the country had expressed their fury; within four months the number had risen to 160. Not only in the four provinces, but also in all the Bantustans (black homelands set up in terms of the policy of separate development) and even in the north of Namibia some form of upheaval was experienced.

Soweto was the epicentre of the revolt, however. Although schools re-opened towards the end of July 1976, and attendance began slowly to increase, the Afrikaans decree having been relaxed in the meantime, many school buildings were only then set on fire, possibly by militants who did not want others to return to school. On 4 August 20 000 students tried to march from the township to police headquarters at John Vorster Square in Johannesburg to demand the release of fellow pupils held in custody since 16 June. The march was stopped by the police.

On the same day the students organised the first of a series of work boycotts by Soweto workers. On 23, 24 and 25 August there was a second stay-away from work, during which migrant workers went on the rampage, attacking and killing other residents, among them schoolchildren. A third stay-away followed on 13, 14 and 15 September.

During demonstrations in several Soweto schools on 17 September against Henry Kissinger's visit to South Africa to discuss the Rhodesian question, six children were shot dead and 35 injured. Six days later schoolchildren held a peaceful demonstration in central Johannesburg. But violence returned to Soweto within a month, when on 17 October a large crowd of angry students destroyed 30 municipal vehicles after the funeral of a schoolboy who had died in police custody shortly after the demonstration in Johannesburg.

Throughout 1977 repeated skirmishes between students and police took place, some resulting in more deaths of students. The students continued to organise protests and demonstrations, and their campaign against Bantu Education grew rather than diminished. Soweto was virtually under martial law and in a state of occupation. Calm was not really restored to the township until the beginning of 1978.

Adapted from John Kane-Berman (1978)
Soweto: Black Revolt, White Reaction,
Johannesburg: Ravan Press, pp. 1–3.

'There were hundreds of students in front of me, and we were marching to the central administrative block in Zone One. That also went up in flames, and it was burnt down. People were killed, they were attacked, not physically, they were told to get out, and that's when I realised that this thing somehow has gotten out of hand.'

This book is constructed from stories told by people about their involvement in the events that took place in Soweto in 1976. They share their memories of that day as well as of the time leading up to it and the days, months and years that followed. They tell their own story in their own words, in their own individual way.

How were the stories elicited? Approximately thirty people were asked a similar set of questions. Their names and brief biographical details appear on pages 183 to 196. Questions asked were wide ranging, yet at the same time focused: What did the respondents remember of their early morning routine on 16 June 1976? What happened on arrival at school? Was there any intimation that something was going to happen? When did things start to change? The intention was to get a detailed description of each person's recollections of 16 June 1976. Respondents were not asked about their political beliefs or the main causes or effects of the uprising.

Each story has been broken up into segments which coincide with the sequence of events on those days: the events which happened before June 16 (Chapter 1); six to eight o'clock on the morning of the 16th (Chapter 2); eight to approximately ten o'clock (Chapter 3); ten o'clock until about two or three o'clock in the afternoon (Chapter 4); about three in the afternoon until midnight (Chapter 5). The Cillie Commission, which was appointed by the then Nationalist government to investigate the uprising and which published its findings in 1979, has been included verbatim as a backdrop to the voices of the students themselves.

For many people, and indeed for the respondents, their stories do not end on June 16. In Chapter 6 respondents tell of the two days that followed, and in Chapter 7, one of the interviewers describes the immediate changes in Soweto brought about by the uprising. Chapter 8 gives a more general idea of how events unfolded in Soweto during the second half of 1976 and during the first two months of 1977. Some background information about the state of black education in the twentieth century is provided in a later chapter. The select bibliography is meant for readers who would like more information about policy, ideology and process around the Soweto uprising.

The interviewees are now adults, yet the voices of the children they were can be heard in the interviews. Some respondents have not spoken much or have never spoken about June 1976. Some were too traumatised to complete the interview, but they welcomed the opportunity to speak in order that their children might know what happened. It is their voices – and their co-operation – that this book records.

The bulk of this book consists of transcripts and translations of these interviews from languages such as Zulu, Venda, English, Tsonga and Sotho. Every effort had been made to transcribe and translate the interviews as accurately as possible. Gandhi Malungane, one of the interviewers who was also responsible for some translations, summarised this approach: 'I listened to what the people were saying. Then I asked myself how they would say that in English, not how I would translate it into English.'

It is hoped that this approach will give respondents and their families pleasure in reading their own story.

TRANSCRIBERS' NOTE

Interviews have been recorded without changes to the grammar or syntax of the spoken word. Where the meaning of sentences may be obscured by the idiosyncrasy of the speaker, words in square brackets have been added. Inaccuracies with regard to times, places, dates, organisations, individuals, etc. were not corrected in transcription. In this book the ellipsis [...] has been used to show that the respondent paused for some or other reason.

Chapter 1
Before 16 June 1976

PHYDIAN MATSEPE, *Orlando High School*

Q: Were you taught in Afrikaans?

Phydian: In 1973 I was doing Form One (Grade Eight). We were taught Maths in Afrikaans – not all subjects were taught in Afrikaans. We had difficulties; even Mr Ntshalintshali, who taught us Rekenkunde, struggled with Afrikaans. Both teachers and learners battled with Afrikaans.

SOLLY MPSHE, *Morris Isaacson High School*

Q: Did you do some subjects in Afrikaans?

Solly: We were doing Agriculture in Afrikaans, we called it Landbou. We did that in Form One (Grade Eight), Form Two (Grade Nine). I am not quite sure if we did Landbou in Form Three (Grade Ten). That was the only subject, all right, that we were doing in Afrikaans, and obviously Afrikaans as a second language. But there was this thing in our minds that – if this whole thing continues – we are going to have problems [with] Afrikaans as a medium of instruction. We used to make it a joke. Like: 'Hey, just imagine now doing Physical Science in Afrikaans; just imagine doing Geography in Afrikaans, if we are having difficulties coping doing the subject in English.'

I don't believe that the whole thing, even if it didn't happen in '76, was going to work. It was not going to work because they were going to be worse off generally. The declining percentage surely was going to

13

be having a bad effect on the department of – whatever they used to call that department of education. And if the authorities were not going to listen, surely the same sort of revolt that they had was going to happen. Maybe we were going to talk of June 16, but in 1977 or '78.

I remember with Landbou, we used to give right answers, but not understanding, you know. I don't think even the teachers were equipped to train students in Afrikaans. In fact there were very few Afrikaans teachers. And even the chap who was giving us Landbou in Afrikaans couldn't teach but was just reading. And he couldn't even explain. Now imagine, we were doing seven subjects, okay, minus vernacular and English, then you are left with five now. Imagine, doing five subjects in a language that you are battling to understand. I mean even the Afrikaans grammar results were showing that always you would have your vernacular, English, then Afrikaans, in that order most of the times.

Now when you say people must learn other subjects in Afrikaans, or all the subjects in Afrikaans, that was a recipe for disaster. I don't know ... the Nats, were they thinking that by doing that, they would sort of be having a good or strong hold on us as their people, or they just didn't give a damn, or their plan was to frustrate all the effort of making an African child better. Until today I am still not clear what was their whole plan. But it was not going to work. If June 16 didn't happen, it was going to happen, especially because they started at primary level. I don't know if they knew that at high school they were going to meet some resistance. If it started working, from one school it would spread gradually to the other primaries, eventually maybe up to secondary level. But we knew that they had a plan, a gradual plan, that would ensure that by the end of so many years every student in Soweto or in South Africa would be learning in Afrikaans.

You were getting an exodus, actually, of students in South Africa to neighbouring countries, that was one way and some of us did that, actually, running away because we were not sure what these guys were really interested in. But those who were going to remain were either going to quit school early, all right, and out of those who would be remaining – surely they were going to revolt against the system.

THOMAS NTULI, *Nghungunyane Junior Secondary School*

Thomas: Ja, right, so that was the cause of the 1976 uprising, because we deny that thing to be used as a medium of instruction. You know why, because we were so confused. They changed the subjects that we were doing in English. Now it was something like Wiskunde, Geskiedenis and all that. We were all confused, we couldn't make it. So the issue of '76, the cause, it was Afrikaans not to be used as a medium of instruction.

You know my main aim was just to pass, progress, to become something in order to help my mom, because she was suffering and all that. We became confused, because of Afrikaans. You see, they changed. They never changed the syllabus from January. They just changed when we were about to write.

Ja, they changed it, you see, Mathematics was now Wiskunde. I was doing History, it was Geskiedenis. So I was doing Biology; it was Biologie. They needed us to translate everything into Afrikaans.

STEVE LEBELO, *Madibane High School*

Steve: We had the two subjects in Form One (Grade Eight): Landbou and Rekenkunde. All students had to do that, except that Landbou was done by us male students. The female students would have been doing Home Economics at the time, and they did it in English. That's odd. But when we went to Form Two (Grade Nine), the government came up with another new ruling. I think we were the first group. We had to have General Science separated into Biology and Physical Science, and this is what they did at Madibane High School. I remember they looked at our results from Form One (Grade Eight) and then gave us an option.

They said: 'Now that you have passed Form One (Grade Eight), you are going into Form Two (Grade Nine), you have to choose the subjects that you want to do.'

Then they gave us two streams of subjects, General and the Science subjects, and they said: 'Those who want to do Mathematics and Science, you know Chemistry and Physics, will go to Room Eight.'

Various people volunteered, and they were in that class. Then they said: 'The balance of you people should do General, but we do think that there are some students amongst you who have the potential to do well

15

in the Sciences, on the basis of your results, and we are going to choose those as the second group of the Science group.'

I happened to have been taken in that lot. I had to do Mathematics again, even though initially I hadn't actually opted for that. So it was on the basis of our performance in Form One (Grade Eight) that we were taken to do Mathematics and Science in Form Two (Grade Nine), but we did that along with History and not Geography. We did that with History and Accounting. Those would have been our four subjects. I think that this is absolutely important, because this was 1974, when I was in Form Two (Grade Nine), and all my subjects were in English. I never had an Afrikaans subject, except doing Afrikaans as a language, but then two years later the government came back again. They had had a review of their 50/50 [English/Afrikaans policy], and they wanted to bring that back, and they began to introduce that very aggressively from 1974. By then it actually wasn't going to affect me, because it was being introduced in the lower levels, and in 1975, I was in Form Three (Grade Ten), and I think that I had escaped the new rule.

Q: So the only subject you had in Afrikaans was Afrikaans?

Steve: Yes, it was Afrikaans. But this was different from what the situation was the year before. In 1973 I did Landbou in Afrikaans, and Rekenkunde, which is Mathematics, in Afrikaans. So in '74 I had all my subjects in English.

Q: And the other kids, how did they manage? Did you notice they were struggling?

Steve: Not really, except that Mathematics would have been a problem. But there were no problems related to mastering subjects because of the language variable. Certainly not in my group.

Q: And the groups below you?

Steve: That's where the problem was, because a year later in 1975, when I was in Form Three (Grade Ten), that's when the government was moving back aggressively to the 50/50 language policy. That's when we began experiencing a lot of problems because [students] would have had to do two of their subjects in Afrikaans, and that was compulsory. They did experience problems with that.

GANDHI MALUNGANE, *Nghungunyane Junior Secondary School*

Q: And which subjects were you taught in Afrikaans?

Gandhi: When everything started, when I came from my primary, I didn't like Afrikaans. But not to say I didn't like it, it was difficult. You see, Arithmetic and Afrikaans were very difficult subjects. When we started, I realised that everything was in Afrikaans now. It became so difficult. Every subject to me started to be difficult.

I remember, we had this old man, an old man, he was a coloured. He was the one we used to call 'Letterkunde, Letterkunde'. So he was sort of speaking this 'suiwer (pure) Afrikaans'. When they started to teach everything in Afrikaans, to me it became very difficult. It became something like French, you know, because I couldn't even understand what was happening.

Q: And did you have to write exams in Afrikaans?

Gandhi: Yes, we had to, because I remember, one test in History, I got three out of one hundred.

To us, going to school, it started as fun, even if it was compulsory, and then we were given a lot of this 'cram' work. We had to recite. Even Arithmetic, we had to recite: it was like 'two plus two', without knowing what it did mean, these recitations. You know that recitation called 'Luilekker', I could recite that, but I didn't know 'Look at the moon, look at the moon'. I didn't know what was English there, what was Afrikaans there. To me it was ... we call it shlungu, it was shlungu.

After I was at Nghungunyane, I started to realise that no, this is Afrikaans, this is English. I started to differentiate now.

DIKELEDI MOTSWENE, *Ithute Junior Secondary School*

Q: What subjects were you doing?

Dikeledi: It was vernac – Sotho, Mathematics ... and it was funny, I was doing Mathematics in Afrikaans. [It was] very difficult. And Afrikaans, English, Biology, Geography, History. In Afrikaans, we were doing Afrikaans as Afrikaans, and we were doing this Arithmetic, in Afrikaans. It was so difficult. The rest we were taught in English.

Q: So you were never taught in your mother tongue?

Dikeledi: No, sometimes they were explaining them. So we switched between English and our mother tongue, Sotho.

17

Q: So it was just Maths and Afrikaans that were taught in Afrikaans?
Dikeledi: Yes, and it was so difficult. You know, we even didn't like the teacher when he came in. It was Mr Madlala. And Mr Madlala, sometimes he feels that we don't like him. It's because, why? We don't understand some of the things, and you know when you are at school, you like to see that you've always got all [things] right, like you have all the stars on your book. To understand and like the subject – but it wasn't like that.

My favourite subject was Science, and Geography and History. I did like those subjects, really.

In fact I was just looking at my books, because I wanted to be something. I wanted to be a scientist. You know why I wanted to be a scientist? I wanted to mix things, but because my parents were not having enough money, I didn't go too far. I dropped.

In May, I think it was May, the students had meetings. Our school, they had a meeting. They were telling us that a person must take the subject that he or she likes. You don't have to take all the subjects. I didn't understand by then what's going on and why do they say that.

They say that you mustn't do Afrikaans. Now we were asking ourselves, why mustn't we do this Afrikaans?

Somebody asked: 'It's because we don't pass Afrikaans. What are we going to do with this Afrikaans? Is it the Afrikaans that's going to make us to go and have work?'

Those were the questions that were being asked and answered.
Q: Were they angry when they were talking about it?
Dikeledi: No, they were not angry. It was like a discussion. There's another school, I don't know if I can remember that school, that came to our school. Our seniors in our school started making groups. Some of these children, when it was time for these subjects, the teacher would come in the class, and then he will come and teach, and nobody will ask questions, nobody will write that Afrikaans.
Q: So they started to boycott Afrikaans in the classroom?
Dikeledi: Yes. It was, by then, it wasn't like they were boycotting it, but they were just telling the teachers: 'We don't understand this language, why do we have to do it?'

Because it wasn't everyone that was taking this Afrikaans, the Maths in Afrikaans. Some they were doing it in English. Now the feeling was, why do we in our school do that? The other school, they were doing it in English. Yes, so the others they were doing it in Afrikaans.

Q: In your school?

Dikeledi: Yes, in our school. When we were looking at that Maths in English, it was easy. Now this name, Rekenkunde, which is in Afrikaans, Maths. On that day, it wasn't all right. They were not feeling all right, that day, it was like … it was just tense. It was before June, mid-May.

Q: What did they do?

Dikeledi: They didn't do anything. They didn't do anything by then, but you can feel that the atmosphere in the class, it is not good. As the teacher now is writing on the blackboard, and nobody is writing. The teachers then, they were very strict.

The teachers were saying: 'Okay, you guys, you don't want to write, I'm giving you the homework. Tomorrow, I want it.'

I went home, and I went to tell the lady with whom I was staying: 'You know, it was funny at school today, we didn't write Afrikaans. The two subjects of Afrikaans and Maths.'

She said: 'Why?'

I said to her: 'I don't know, and I feel ashamed not to write that subject, because the teacher did give it to us, and even the teacher is going to punish us tomorrow.'

These other students said to me: 'You mustn't write.'

So we didn't know whether we must write it or we mustn't write it.

She said: 'It's up to somebody to do it. If you understand it and you like it, you can write it.'

So the feeling was, nobody is understanding it, so if you write it, you are meaning you understand it.

The next day, we have to come back, and when we come back, when that period comes, the teacher punished us all, because we didn't write. I didn't do the homework, I'm afraid to do the homework, because these others didn't do it.

Q: So you didn't know who to listen to really?

Dikeledi: No, really. We were punished. I said to them: 'I'm not going to do punish[ment] again.'

Q: How did they punish you?

Dikeledi: Shoo, it was bad! With a cane. On the hands, it was terrible. That's why I didn't like to be punished. So we had to be punished by cane, and the girls had to clean the classroom, and the boys had to look [after] the gardens. We had gardens at our school. And you have to go late, you have to go home late, because now we are punished.

That passed, and then we didn't continue to boycott. We feel that, why should we, let's carry on, if we fail Afrikaans, and pass these others, we will still pass. That was the idea we did have by then. First week, June, there was this high school, we had to [meet] with them for sports. There we heard now: 'Really, really guys, we are going to boycott this Bantu Education.'

With me, I didn't think it was something that is going to cause such a big thing.

I just thought: 'Okay, we're boycotting. We have to boycott this Afrikaans, and then the teacher who is teaching us this Afrikaans is not going to teach us.'

That was the idea I could get by then. It was bad.

TULU MHLANGA, *Tiakeni Junior Primary School*

Q: Tell me about Afrikaans at school, were you aware?

Tulu: No, no, no, I was not aware of that. I was only told by my mother that there is a language which was not needed by the students. She even told me how she used to dodge Afrikaans period during her school-days. She told me that she used to poke her nose with her fingers, then blood would come out. Then she would be excused from class for that period. To me Afrikaans did not affect me to such an extent that I could know that it was the cause of all that fight.

DINGANE LEBELE, *Madibane High School*

Q: Coming to Afrikaans, did you have a problem with it?

Dingane: I did not have a problem with Afrikaans. Besides, it was compulsory to do Afrikaans. It is not that I liked it. It was part of our curriculum. You could not say you did not like it. Pupils who were against it were in Orlando West.

Q: You were coping with it?

20

Dingane: Yes, I was coping very well with Afrikaans. That is why I say I recited the poem 'Muskiete-jag'. I did not worry about Afrikaans.

ERICK NGOBENI, *Nghungunyane Junior Secondary School*

Q: Did you know then that the fight was involving the Afrikaans issue?

Erick: I really did not know. To me it was just a combination of a fight and happiness. I did not know what we were fighting for. I started to understand what was happening very late. Somewhere around July and August.

HENDRICK TSHABALALA, *Gazankulu Senior Primary School*

Q: Did you know that there was a change to Afrikaans as a medium of instruction?

Hendrick: Ja, I was aware of this thing called Afrikaans which was to be a medium of instruction to all the subjects. I knew it because we were also taught Afrikaans but not in all languages. Like the reason for the strike, for instance that they don't want to learn Maths, History, Biology in Afrikaans. I just heard of that later. Immediately after we were released from school, the following day, I heard from others that the reason why these students [cause] this havoc is because of this thing, it is because of the fact that these people don't want to write Maths in Afrikaans and History in Afrikaans and also Biology in Afrikaans. We learnt the other subjects like Maths in English.

MARTHA MATTHEWS, *Kelekitso Junior Secondary School*

Q: How did the students feel about Afrikaans?

Martha: I am sure that there were already school meetings held against the Afrikaans issue. It was bad, because we did Afrikaans, we were doing Maths, we did it in Afrikaans. We did History in Afrikaans, we did this Business Economics in Afrikaans. We did most of the subjects in Afrikaans, straight, straight. I did not like Afrikaans at all. I [was] just bound to go to school. The subjects were more difficult when they were done in Afrikaans.

STEVE LEBELO, *Madibane High School*

Steve: I attended a meeting on the 13th June, about June 16th, Orlando. I never actually went into the hall, but I knew about the meeting and we did go, out of curiosity. It was also because my brother was a member of the South African Student's Movement (SASM) at the time, and he was two years older than me and we spent a lot of time together. In fact we talked about the coming march of June 16th, and he told me what SASM had actually planned, and I think he also informed me about the meeting on Sunday 13th, where the Student's Representative Council was actually formed. On Tuesday 15th, not very many students, but a couple of students, and I was one of those, gathered around street corners. I do remember on the Soweto Highway, next to Immink Drive, a couple of students stood there and told people about the march the next day.

In fact we were actually doing the telling! At some point, me and a couple of guys, about five, six, we were at the four-way stops, where a lot of people got off buses and taxis, and we just explained to them that the next day, June 16th, a march has been planned for Orlando Stadium. We were all going to congregate at the stadium, and we were going to talk to students about problems, especially relating to the use of Afrikaans. But I don't think that there was a clear kind of plan as to what was going to happen. The idea was that students would meet in a kind of mass meeting, and that perhaps they would be able to take decisions there. I don't think it would have worked anyway, but that's what we had in mind.

VUSI ZWANE, *Rhulane Senior Primary*

Q: What happened on the 15th?

Vusi: We were already in the classrooms. Inspector Mahuhushe was supposed to come and address the senior students of our school, those who were doing Form One (Grade Eight) to Form Three (Grade Ten), because that is the time when I was doing Standard Five (Grade Seven). So [some] people, as they knew the inspector was supposed to come, they locked the gates. When the inspector arrived he found that the gates were locked. He tried to force his way inside the schoolyard. They threw stones at him. He went to the police station to tell them what was happening. So when he came back he found that all the schoolchildren were outside the schoolyard, because our school had a short fence. The gate was locked but they managed to jump [over] and went to the other side of the schoolyard, at the shops. That is where they started looting the delivery vans like bread cars, cooldrink cars and milk cars. The school knocked off at the same time and we were told to come back on the following day, which is June 16th. According to my own calculation this thing started on the 15th.

DAN MOYANE, *Morris Isaacson High School*

Q: How did you know what was going to happen, on the 16th?

Dan: Okay, do you remember, at Belle Primary, they burnt their books. Was it late '75 or early '76? That thing was a small incident, they burnt Afrikaans books, they didn't want to be taught in Afrikaans. We took all the books like Geskiedenis which is History, ja, Wiskunde, they burnt those books, it was a big thing, they called School Board meetings and stuff. Then we knew about that, okay, but weeks before, we used to have students' meetings at school where we would meet and discuss. We were informed that there are plans for schools to express their opposition to Afrikaans. Ja, you know, things were being talked about, March, April.

That week of June 16th, or the week before, we were told that [there] is going to be a meeting at school. And we were only told the day before, on the 15th of June in the afternoon. We were called to assembly by the principal and Tsietsi [Mashinini] addressed us. He told us there had been a meeting and this is what's going to happen.

Q: Was Tsietsi elected leader of the students at that time?

Dan: Not at that time, there had been no elections of any organisation.

Q: How did he assume that position?

Dan: He was very eloquent, he was head of our debating society. I was one of the junior members of the Morris Isaacson High School Debating Society.

Q: A hippy as well at that time?

Dan: Ja, he was a hippy, with a 'skull-cap', with bell-bottoms, a rebel, yes, and at the school he was a natural choice to be a spokesperson. It just happened. There were no elections. But, when the elections for the Student's Representative Council (SRC) [came], he was elected. I don't know where [the idea came from], that the schools must have representa-

23

tives. It's better that students must have a body to represent them, okay, and they match the people, sort of. The next SRC representative was Kgotso, and he was elected by the SRC that was in existence, and he came to every SRC, to every school, to introduce himself as the new thing.

In our school we had elected Tsietsi Maleho. He's still around; he was there because he was also very eloquent and good. But he was not as charismatic as Tsietsi Mashinini. There was also the likes of Kingdom and Murphy Morobe, and we formed a group of ten at school. I was one of the members of the first Group of Ten. It was myself, Kingdom, Matthew, I can't remember the names of the other guys, and we used to meet every day at the end of the school. We would sit by the hedge, hide, and then talk about things quietly, what we were going to do and stuff like that. And then they would take it, Tsietsi would then take it to the SRC, that at Morris people feel like this. I remember things were very quiet.

1. 2001: One group of students who were to meet marchers from schools elsewhere in Soweto at Orlando Stadium, started from Morris Isaacson High School in White City Jabavu. Tsietsi Mashinini, who was to become one of the leading figures of the uprising, was a prefect at this school and helped to organise the march. Photo: Themba Maseko

2. 2001: Madibane High School, Diepkloof, was one of the few senior secondary schools in Soweto where students helped to organise the marches of 16 June 1976. Abe Lebelo, late brother of Steve Lebelo, one of the authors of this book, was enrolled here. Photo: Themba Maseko

3. 2001: Students at the Nghungunyane Secondary School in Chiawelo took an active part in the uprising. It was one of the first ethnically exclusive schools in Soweto for Tsonga-speaking students. Founded in the early seventies, it became a centre for the uprising in the townships south of Old Potchefstroom Road. The spelling on the school building differs from the regular spelling of the name of the school. Photo: Themba Maseko

4. 2001: Hector Peterson was enrolled at Belle Primary School which lay directly on the route followed by students to Orlando Stadium. A junior secondary school at the time, its students would be affected by the new ruling that subjects such as Mathematics and Biology should be taught through medium of Afrikaans. Photo: Themba Maseko

5. 2001: The students at this school in Chiawelo too were closely involved in the uprising. Thomas Ntuli recalls that on 16 June 'From Vuwani Senior Secondary we went to Sekano-Ntoane organising all the students. We said: "Pens down, books down."' Photo: Themba Maseko

4

5

Chapter 2
Early morning: Wednesday, 16 June 1976

DAN MOYANE, *Morris Isaacson High School*

Dan: We were asked not to make our parents aware, so it [was] a normal morning, in fact, my mother was like: 'Hey, child, here's money for bread. When you come back, eat!'

No problem, no problem – the usual things, so I didn't raise any suspicions. I tried my best, which was fine. So when they left to catch their bus to Nancefield and train to work, I took my placard. It was there ... we weren't taking books, but they had seen my bag, it was sitting there.

Q: For them, it was a normal day?

Dan: Yes, for them I was going to school. When they left, I then took it to the bedroom, my books and everything. I was in uniform, I had my tie on [and] everything else, and I went.

It was exciting to walk to school that day because we were going [to do] something very important, very big. We had never done it before but we were going to do it. I walked [with] other guys, everybody, seeing other people, very quietly, and this placard of mine.

DINGANE LEBELE, *Madibane High School*

Q: Can you tell me what your expectations were when you woke up on the morning of 16 June 1976?

Dingane: I did not know anything. I did not expect what happened. I was surprised by the unrest that followed. This thing of June 16, I did not expect. In fact June 16 did not start on the 16th here in Diepkloof. 'Power' here in Diepkloof started on the 17th. Elsewhere in Soweto it started on the 17th.

PRISCILLA MSESENYANE, *St Matthews School*

Priscilla: When I woke up on June 16, 1976, I heard noises outside. My mother was preparing to go to work. We were told not to go to school as a few days before there had been signs of unrest. Some older students from Morris Isaacson came to our school to convey that message. They warned that if we went to school we might get hurt. She [my mother] also agreed that we stay home.

ERICK NGOBENI, *Nghungunyane Junior Secondary School*

Erick: I woke up, as usual, like all the other days. I ate soft porridge, because it was our usual breakfast, since bread was scarce at that time. After that, I took my books. I usually left home at half past seven, because our school was a little far away. I went to collect my friend who stayed nearby. He was called Ronald Rikhotso. Then we went to school just like the other days.

GANDHI MALUNGANE, *Nghungunyane Junior Secondary School*

Gandhi: You know, when it comes to breakfast, that's going to be a simple thing, because it was like every morning, we had soft porridge. Every morning before going to school, we had soft porridge, because we couldn't afford bread. When it comes to clothing, what did I wear? Black and white. Because we were wearing black trouser, or grey, again white or blue. So my favourite was black and white.

I had this friend, Themba Madingane, who stayed next to me. And there was one called Gideon, and they are still there today. We used to call on each other going to school. So, that day, it happened the same way, I left early in the morning. Quarter to eight was exactly when everything started, because it's wintertime. Summertime it was exactly half past seven.

It was winter, so we used to hold these stones. We used to put them inside the stove and then they get warm. Not inside the stove, there

28

was this ... like a tray where ashes could fall. So we'd put it there. So my sister had to put her stone there, or my brother has his stone, just like that. In the morning one would take out his [stone] – sometimes there was this fight! So I took mine, wrapping it with paper and going straight to Themba, taking Gideon, because it's less than a kilo from my place to school, it's not far. You can see the school, it's only that there are houses in front, you can see the school from where I stay.

So I collected Themba and we went to Gideon, down to school. So it was plus minus half past seven, you see, because we made sure that [at] quarter to eight we were at school. Ja, I collected my friends and we walked to school.

SAM ZIKHALI, *Ibhongo Junior Secondary School*
Q: When you woke up on the morning of 16 June 1976, was there a sign that it was going to any different to other days?
Sam: There was nothing wrong, nothing showing, nothing sinister. We all went to school. We were writing exams, half-yearly exams, and during the day the teachers ... actually, something went wrong outside. We were still writing and they said we must all go home. Then we went home; that's when we saw how cars were being burnt and everything [was] going wrong. When we were at home we started joining the groups and we went back on a rampage. We burnt cars, threw stones.
Q: When did all this start?
Sam: About ten, eleven. The teachers told us to leave. We must all leave and we must all go home. I saw that people are fighting, because they were throwing stones and we all hated the white people and so we went.

It came to my knowledge that we were throwing stones at Putco buses and at all the [company] cars. I joined everybody who was throwing stones right up until I got home and then changed my clothes and I joined them. I was moving with others, any group, to the bottle stores, to the bars, and doing all this stone throwing.

STEVE LEBELO, *Madibane High School*
Steve: It started with the usual thing. Normally, I'd be up about six o'clock, and I took turns with my brother, who washed first. At the time we didn't have a bathroom; we'd have these plastic bath-tubs. We used to

29

call them 'sijana', which means a dish, because it's shaped like a dish, but we used that for washing [and] we'd take turns. Whoever washed first, would have to go and buy bread once they had finished washing, bread and milk, and we had that for breakfast, a couple of slices of bread and tea. Normally it was tea with milk, which is why we had to go and buy bread and milk in the morning. [The shop] used to be close by, but now when I look at it ... well, let's say a kilo, a kilo and a half away from home. We had our breakfast and we both left the house.

THOMAS NTULI, *Nghungunyane Junior Secondary School*

Thomas: Nothing exactly happened when I woke up early in the morning. It was something that I encountered at school. I mean, I was used to that procedure: wake up, wash my body, wear the uniform and be punctual at school. It was in me. I never had my breakfast before I went to school, because Nghungunyane was near to my place. I [would] just run home, have two slices of bread, and drink tea, black tea.

[June 16th] is something that happened at school. God knows, what exactly happened there is something we never planned ... something we never planned. I mean, [it] simultaneously just happened and it became what it is today.

GEORGE BALOYI, *Nghungunyane Junior Secondary School*

Q: How was the day when you woke up?
George: They were similar to the other ones because we left to [go to] school with our books for learning. At school we were in at half past seven and we were out at half past four. On the 16th we were in at half past seven, but we knocked off at twelve.

ERIC NKUNA, *St Matthews School*

Eric: As a Catholic school we used to attend church services in addition to the normal classes. Wednesday was mainly a church day. I used to pick up a friend of mine every morning on our way to school. Our parents told us not to go to school on the 16th as they worried that there was going to be trouble. My parents told me so. My mother actually told me. I did not go to school on the 16th. When I woke up there was already trouble. There was shooting and burning and looting.

MARTHA MATTHEWS, *Kelekitso Junior Secondary School*

Q: How was 16 June 1976 from the time you woke up in the morning?

Martha: It looked like a dangerous day. Immediately, when we woke up, there was smoke coming out towards Dube. When you are at home and looked towards where the taxis are, when you looked at Deep Soweto, there was smoke. You could see and feel that some things were burning. Meanwhile at Meadowlands things were not yet started, but [on] that side of Zone Five they had already started with the likes of bottle stores and all that.

Q: Did you see any trouble on your way to school?

Martha: The problem was there because those children who woke up earlier than us, they were now coming back. There were people who phoned to various schools. They were actually notified to go back home.

Q: Did you reach the school?

Martha: No, I did not reach the school. We just group ourselves. [It was] from eight o'clock.

JOYCE MAKHUBELE, *Tiakeni Junior Primary School*

Joyce: We woke up very well and washed ourselves, ate soft porridge, we wore our uniform. We then went to the same Tiakeni [Junior Primary School]. In fact the school was not far from my home.

Q: Did any friend accompany you to school on the 16th?

Joyce: I can't remember well, but I think I was with Josephina, and the likes of Thoko, because those were the people I went with every day.

Q: Was there any sign of danger in the morning of 16 June?

Joyce: No. Things were not showing that it will be dangerous. There was no problem.

VICTOR BUTHELEZI, *Lilydale Senior Primary School*

Victor: We did the normal things. Woke up in the morning and then went to school.

HENDRICK TSHABALALA, *Gazankulu Senior Primary School*

Hendrick: I woke up very well and washed myself all right. I took my books and went straight to the gate where I waited for my friends. They came and we pulled each other to school.

Ja, I still remember them even now. Even now I still meet some of them. Who were they? Ephraim Mbhokota, Daniel Shiluvane, Raphael Bila, and then Dennis Sono, and the late Alex Chabangu and Clive Mbhalati and Dizuti Shakoane. We were next to each other.

Q: Who used to collect whom first?

Hendrick: I am staying by the school side and they stay a little far from school. So they collected each other and then together they collected me. So I can say they collected me last, and then we met together and went up to school.

KEDI MOTSAU, *Naledi High School*

Kedi: I can't remember breakfast because I was excited. We were told the previous day: 'Tomorrow is going to be a strike' – actually, not a strike: 'We are going to march to a certain place, somewhere in Orlando West.' Then the next day, June 16th, we went to school, and the weather, it was windy, and it was fine, really sunny.

[It was a] normal day, normal day at school, at eight, because I was just near to the school, it was about five to eight.

DIKELEDI MOTSWENE, *Ithute Junior Secondary School*

Dikeledi: On June 16th, I just woke up as usual. It was at about seven a.m. In fact I woke up at six a.m., and at seven a.m. I was preparing myself and having breakfast. We didn't have bathrooms, I was taking the water with which I was washing myself, outside. Yes! It was cold.

So, I heard the other girl, Nthabiseng, calling me. She said: 'Dikeledi, Dikeledi!'

I said: 'Yes!'

She said: 'You are left behind!'

I asked: 'But why? It's still early.'

She said: 'No, you don't know! Today we are not going to school!'

I said: 'Why? Yesterday we were at school. Now why today are we not going to school?'

She said: 'Don't take your school-bag, don't take your lunch. We have to just go to school.'

I said: 'Why?'

She said: 'You'll see!'

I said: 'Okay, let me just turn the radio off and lock the house so that I can come. Just wait for me, I'm coming.'

I was having my uniform on, so I was thinking, Must I take my school-bag? What must I do?

I was just confused, really I was confused.

I took my school-bag, I went out, closed the door and Nthabiseng said: 'No! Leave your school-bag, your books will be lost.'

I said: 'Why?'

She said: 'They said we are going to march.'

I'm going back, and I'm taking my school-bag into the house. I said: 'No, I'm not going to wear my school shoes.' I changed my school shoes, and I put on the tackies. How are we going to march?

I said: 'I'm not going to take my uniform. What if there's a problem? They are going to identify us.'

So I just put [on] my tackies, and then I took my hat and put it on. It was a little bit chilly that day, but I didn't take my jersey, I just took my black and white uniform and then we went. We saw the other kids, busy running.

Top: 2001: As it runs from Mofolo Village up the hill to Dube, Mahalafele Road today still provides a major link between the western and the eastern Soweto townships to the north of Old Potchefstroom Road. It was on this road that young students joyously set out on the march in 1976 which, when they reached Orlando West, turned from a demonstration into a violent confrontation with the police. Photo: Themba Maseko

Bottom: 2001: Regina Mundi Catholic Church on Old Potchefstroom Road seen from the east. Situated close to the intersection with Old Roodepoort Road, the church became an important landmark in Soweto during the struggle against apartheid. Since it is the largest church in Soweto, scores of political funerals and other political gatherings were staged here. Photo: Themba Maseko

Top: 2001: In the heat of the clash with the authorities, some students managed to slip through the police barricade. They rushed down the hill in Orlando West, went through the Klipspruit valley and escaped by way of the subway under the railway line to Orlando Stadium. Photo: Themba Maseko

Bottom: 2001: Orlando Stadium, here seen from outside, was the ultimate destination of the young demonstrators on 16 June 1976. However, the march was stopped in Orlando West at an intersection not far from Phefeni Station at what is today known as Hector Peterson Square. Hector Peterson, the 13-year-old boy who was the first to die on that day, has became synonomous with the Soweto uprising through the famous photograph taken by Sam Nzima showing a distraught young man carrying Hector's limp body, with his sister running alongside. Photo: Themba Maseko

WEDNESDAY, 16 JUNE 1976
West Rand: Soweto

07h00: According to a woman reporter from a local newspaper, who had received information concerning a planned protest march, all was quiet at the Naledi High School grounds and there were no pupils about.

07h45: Col. J.A. Kleingeld, Station Commander of the Orlando Police Station, ordered all available policemen to be on stand-by. A Black sergeant who was sent to inspect the area saw several groups of marchers. The march was proceeding along Xorile Street from north to south. The sergeant notified the Orlando Police Station that children were marching in the streets.

Chapter 3
Arrival at school until about ten o'clock

GANDHI MALUNGANE, *Nghungunyane Junior Secondary School*

Gandhi: I left early in the morning. I collected my friends and we walked to school. As usual, before the bell rings, we used to play. I didn't like playing soccer before, but [it] was my new hobby. We stayed there and talked, everyone was talking. Surprisingly, you know, until eight o'clock, the bell never rang.

Q: Was that unusual?

Gandhi: Very unusual. But we never realised what was happening. You know, when the bell didn't ring, it was a pleasure to us, but past eight, the bell had to ring, and then we all went to the assembly. Assembly: it was surprising, because there were only a few teachers in assembly. We just prayed, but there was no preaching. Normally one teacher there [would] stand up, talking, preaching, reading the Bible, after that praying. After that the principal would come and talk about what is bad, what is not bad.

But that day it never happened. After praying the Lord's Prayer, in chorus, we were all dismissed to the classes. But still there were no teachers. You know, when the teacher's not in the classroom, there's noise, all those things, playing, playing, playing. We do this, exactly, on the attitude that the teacher might be coming, jumping up there, you must be careful that you don't play far away from your desk.

But that day, the teachers never came, until after a few periods. So now, after a short break, there were these students forming groups, and the teachers tried to dismiss them from forming those groups.

They were students from another school who came there, you see, to call the students in my school. So they went there, addressing them about (although I heard that later) a meeting. We heard that there was going to be a meeting at Orlando Stadium, and some of them [said]: 'We are going to hand over a memorandum. The students are going to hand over a memorandum.'

Some [were] saying: 'Okay, the students are going to the police stations.'

Immediately after, we went back to school, to the class.

It was roughly ten, somewhere [around] ten, because our first break was at half past ten.

Q: So the students spoke to you and then they left?

Gandhi: No, they didn't. I don't know ... There are these ignorant people like myself, who were young. But then when these other students, these older students, went there in that group, in that meeting there, I saw the teachers trying to dismiss them. We never took notice of that. But immediately after they left, then there came these students of our school, who said: 'No, there's this and this and this and this; we've got to go.'

They just simply said: 'We are marching to meet other students somewhere in Soweto, and then we are going to Orlando Stadium.'

We had to join. They just said: 'Let's go, let's go,' to everyone, and then we joined.

DAN MOYANE, *Morris Isaacson High School*

Dan: We walked up to Morris [Isaacson High School], because I lived in White City [and] it was not far. I used to walk every day. I got to school and the buzz was different. It was like, hey, there were talks, what's happening?

And the principal had been told. I think overnight, the likes of Tsietsi had already [been] informed and Kgotso, and Enos Naledi had told the principal. So our principal was Mr Mathabathe – he had been informed, very good and well in education.

He called us to assembly and did the normal thing and he welcomed everything, said: 'I know it's not a normal day today.' He knew what

[was] happening. He explained his support for the thing: 'Go well and behave, good luck and we are behind you.'

And the buzz there ... ah, that means we live now, wow.

We [were] told that other children will come from the west, will be coming to join us along that road, like those from Central Western Jabavu. When you go down to Sizwe Stores, next to Mama Sally Motlana – we would go down there towards the golf course, which is now a squatter camp. We marched there, and people from Orlando West, Orlando North, Diepkloof would come that way, towards the railway, and our meeting point is going to be Orlando Stadium. So that briefing was given and we must keep behaving and sing. And start singing the songs: 'Thina sizwe ... Sikhalela' (We the nation ... Are weeping).

SOLLY MPSHE, *Morris Isaacson High School*

Q: Tell me about the morning of 16 June 1976.

Solly: We went to school ... there was no sign [of anything] whatsoever. At eight o'clock we went to assembly and thereafter went to the classroom. I think things started happening just before nine o'clock, during the second period. Remember, periods used to last for 45 minutes. Ja, quarter to nine, just before nine or thereabout. Schoolkids from Naledi High ... there was a school which was called Derateng at that time – I think it became Thomas Mofolo later. I don't know what they call it nowadays. They all came in and forced us out of the classes and we didn't know what was happening, to be honest. And we [were] forced to join the march. We only realised from the placards when we went out that it has to do with Afrikaans as a medium of instruction. And it was like we were marching.

VUSI ZWANE, *Rhulane Senior Primary School*

Vusi: When we arrived at school, that is when the trouble started. Because when the bell rang at eight o'clock, we used to be addressed by the principal, but that day the principal was told not to take the platform. Then Murphy Morobe was introduced to us. He then started to tell us about the Afrikaans issue.

Ja, because from January ... even though it was not that serious, it was already introduced. Maths was called Wiskunde and Biology

39

was called Biologie. Geography ... Even now I forget its Afrikaans name.

But on the 16th we were addressed by Murphy Morobe. Murphy Morobe told us that we must behave ... we must behave well. We must be quiet. We went to Elkah Stadium to meet the students from the other schools. When we arrived there ... I think it was something past ten to eleven. I am just estimating the time. And then we were introduced to Tsietsi Mashinini whom we did not know. He was just a young boy. Because he was short he had to climb on top of a tree so that we could see him clearly. He told us about what was happening ...

BAFANA HLATSWAYO, *Nonto Junior Primary School*

Q: Tell me about your usual morning procedures.

Bafana: When I went to school my habit was to use a double-up. There were a lot of double-ups and fences, short fences on most of the yards. There was no high fence whatsoever. So we used to jump fences to various yards.

We always walked in groups when I went to school. One of my friends – I remember we used to call him Zondi. His surname was Buthelezi. He was my close friend, much close.

On the 16th of June, we walked just normal hours. We went to school as [if] it [was] just a normal day. There was nothing. We even learnt well, though we were a little disturbed on our lessons. It was after ten or to eleven, somewhere there. Something unusual happened because we used to knock off at two, but that day we knocked off early. We asked ourselves what was happening and, at the same time, we were happy to go home early that day.

Q: How were your lessons disturbed?

Bafana: Oh well, I would not say that we were disturbed but we were so excited to knock off early at school. There is nothing that disturbed us or that made us aware of the fact that there would be something, no.

If I can remember well, we were told by the principal. We were not used to because at times a certain mistress [female teacher] would come and ring the bell and we would knock off, but at that [time] he did not want any explanation or whatever.

The bell [rang]. Tilo, tilo, tilo!

40

He just told us: 'Out.'

Oh! Just like that. We were shocked and happy. Happy to go home that early.

Q: No one entered your school to talk to the principal?

Bafana: Our school was a very a strict school, we were also neat, it was also neat. You know why? We had a very strict principal, and another thing, it was in a very exposed area. That means it was on Old Potchefstroom Road and next to Moroka police station. [In] such [a] school you made sure that everything that was happening inside must not give the people who are outside the impression of what is happening inside, because if you can be seen or you are a wrong person, very quick there would be police or security to find out as to what was happening. So there were alarms and all those things by then.

So people did arrive, but as schoolchildren we were never aware what were these people doing at our school. You understand I can't suspect these people came in disguise, as they knew the kind of place they were going to. That is why they never exposed themselves and also they did not disturb us.

JOYCE MAKHUBELE, *Tiakeni Junior Primary School*

Joyce: Things became wrong when we arrived at school. We reached school and sung. We prayed and went to the classes. We just heard noise outside. Then one mistress came and informed us that there was a bakery which was burnt down and bread taken at the side of Nghungunyane. They then said we should go home. There was singing, some said 'Ho-ho!' Some were talking; it was a confusion. I can't remember [the songs], but one of them was the one which says 'Senzeni na' (What have we done).

In our classroom we were told by mistress Mnisi, she said: 'They say we must go home.' She also told us that there is a burnt bakery at Nghungunyane. She told us that the order [to go home] came from the boys who came to our school. I did not know them. I only knew those who were my schoolmates at Tiakeni and happened to mix with these boys and follow after them. I went through the small gate next to the toilets [at the school]. Then to the street behind the school to Mange Street and went home.

41

HENDRICK TSHABALALA, *Gazankulu Senior Primary School*

Hendrick: We arrived at school and went to assembly. After assembly when we entered the classrooms ... who was that, by the way? First period, before it even got finished, they were already with us, they already arrived, they came from the secondaries.

They then started: 'Hey ... Hey ... Hey ... Hayi ... Hayi ... Hayi ... Hayi ... Release the children and let them go home to stay.'

It was asked what was happening, and they said: 'Don't ask what is happening, let these children go home to stay.'

Well, stupid as we were, we were let out then, it was like the school was out.

Q: When you arrived at school, whom did the secondary students approach?

Hendrick: On their arrival they went straight in the direction of the principal's office. Some were carrying sticks and they were busy singing. Only the elder or senior, I can call them that ...? I can say those leaders. The way I saw them they arrived peacefully. Ja, they all entered. There was not a single one who stood on the street.

The way they were talking to the principal – because we even peeped through the windows – there were no signs of, say, finger-pointing at the principal, no. The way we saw things, although at a distance, they were talking well to the principal.

Hey, I did not know the faces which were there. I didn't know them, they were even wearing different uniforms. It was different schools. So you could not understand which uniform belonged to which school. In fact it was not higher primary or lower primary uniform. Ja, it belonged to seniors only.

Q: Were you not afraid or frightened when this mob entered your school premises?

Hendrick: Well, it was just a mixture of feelings. We were frightened because we did not know what these people were coming for, whether they were coming to kill the principal or for something, we did not know.

Q: Do you remember the song they were singing when they came to your school?

Hendrick: No, that one I can't remember. It was not the likes of 'Kill the boers' or what. It was another one which was sung in Zulu. To me, they were new.

Q: How did you feel about the songs?

Hendrick: I was not feeling good about these songs. No matter how hard I tried to listen to [the songs], I could not understand their meaning.

DIKELEDI MOTSWENE, *Ithute Junior Secondary School*

Dikeledi: Yes, we went to school. When we get there it was just ten to eight. It was just me and my friend. Now we were passing some of the other students on our way, but the feeling of the children, now the others are running, the others are tying themselves with the cloth, and it was like it was a sports day.

We went into school. We didn't go to assembly that day because there was a man standing there and the teachers were just ... they didn't know what was going on. There were people who were coming outside of our school who are like monitoring the schools and telling the students: 'Don't go in ... Stand there.'

Those were leaders, by then, I think. We didn't know them, I didn't know them, who are they, those people. They were ordering people, you see: 'Don't go into your school. Stand there. Go there.' You see.

Some, they were listening to them, and like our school, they did listen, but not exactly.

They wanted to ask the man: 'Why should we go there?'

We were standing there, looking at this man. I think it was just after eight, they were there, the other schools, coming to us, to our school. There were so many of them. I was shocked, I was very shocked by then. I was nervous, in fact. I didn't know what was happening, what was going to happen.

It was like I'm feeling dizzy, and I was just taking Nthabiseng [with] my hand. I don't like crowds, and I was just shocked. Now the problem on that day, people were just running around, running, running, running, going up and down, all over. We didn't know where we were going to, because now people are just running to and fro, to and fro.

ERICK NGOBENI, *Nghungunyane Junior Secondary School*

Erick: When we did what we have done at assembly, we dismissed. At eight o'clock we usually started our lesson, but our school started at half past seven. But in winter it started at twenty to eight. Ultimately we sat at school, just like other days.

Just as we were seated in the classroom as usual, we saw people coming [who] were zabalaza [toyi-toying], they were busy dancing themselves. On arrival they entered in the principal's office. They seemed to be talking peacefully to the principal.

Q: You were talking about the word 'zabalaza'. Did you know the word at that time?

Erick: Ah ... this word 'zabalaza'. I didn't know this word 'zabalaza'. I came to know it now that I am a grown up, after this event of June 16 happened.

Q: What was this group doing when they came to your school?

Erick: They were singing. If I can remember well, the song which they came singing, they were saying: 'Oliver Tambo theta noBotha akhulule, uMandela, Oliver Tambo, akhulule uMandela.' (Oliver Tambo, speak to Botha, so that he must release Mandela.)

Q: Were these songs familiar to you?

Erick: These songs which were sung – I didn't know anything. It was for the first time that I heard this kind of songs. I felt very great [about these songs], although I didn't know them. On hearing them I felt inspired. When I heard them singing, I wished I could go outside to sing with them and ultimately dance together and go wherever they wanted us to go.

Immediately after they entered, they approached the principal. After that I noticed that all the schoolchildren were outside and busy dancing with the group that was singing in the schoolyard. Yes, I also went outside and danced. When we went and danced, they tried a little to stop us, to say: 'Hey, hey ...'

But they found that there was not time, the way things were happening, because it was so crowded outside. Then we went outside and mixed together with the others. There was no way that [the teachers] could identify us; we ultimately left them standing.

Many of this group were our age, some were young. It was a group of different ages, but they were not [very] old. Those [students] whom we were with, those who came to talk to the principal and request that the school must be off, they are also those who went with us outside the schoolyard and we started toyi-toying.

GEORGE BALOYI, *Nghungunyane Junior Secondary School*

George: We went to assembly and everything was right. The principal and teachers addressed [us] just like the other days and we went to classes. The lessons went normal like other days.

There came [these] four boys. I don't know their names. They were coming from Musi High [School] in Pimville. They were coming from there. They are the ones who told us that we must knock off because there was Black Power. They went to the principal, Mr Tlakula. They entered the office. We just saw them calling us. Then we went to assembly and we were told that there was Black Power, we were no more supposed to learn Afrikaans. We must make sure that Afrikaans is done away with.

THOMAS NTULI, *Nghungunyane Junior Secondary School*

Thomas: I was a student at Nghungunyane in 1976, I was fifteen years old at the time. I was doing Form One (Grade Eight). You get me? So right, during the confusion in the classes, we saw a mob coming, mob of students, amongst the students there was Tsietsi Mashinini. I know him facially, you get me, my brother. So you know what happened at my age, I was still a toddler and all that, I never understood what was happening. So we were addressed by Tsietsi and the other colleague, I can't even remember his name. But he filled the books of history.

So what happened? We were told what to do and what not to do. Then we left Nghungunyane. We never regarded [Tsietsi Mashinini] as a prominent figure or leader or whatever. He was just a normal student. I mean he was sort of like a prefect at school, you know a chief prefect, maybe, [we] regarded him in that way. Now they introduced [the] thing of the Student's Representative Council and all that.

We came out of the yard of the school. We saw a van. I've just told you what happened. We attacked those people, those policemen.

Q: When you went to collect students from the other schools, were there leaders who led you?

45

Thomas: No, they were not leaders exactly. We were expected to be ruled by the chief prefect. When we go to each and every school the chief prefect was there, the Tsietsis and the likes.

Q: Was your group led by Tsietsi?

Thomas: Tsietsi and our chief prefect. We had a chief prefect at school. His name was Khinsile. He went to exile, but now he came back. He is within Umkhonto we Sizwe (MK) and all that. He is a general. Thailane was also our co-student, who also went ... I can quote about eleven people that I know and my brother was also involved.

KEDI MOTSAU, *Naledi High School*

Kedi: We went to the school and joined with other schools, marching in the street, collecting other schools on our way down to our destination. I think it was the Orlando Stadium, I'm not sure, because we were not well informed.

We were not told: 'This is what we are going to do.'

It was like: 'We are going to this place, we are going to discuss about this thing, and then hand over a memo to the police.'

So that was it, but there was no procedure. There were leaders who were supposed to lead us to that place. We were not given the route. Yes, most of them were from our school, some of them from other schools.

STEVE LEBELO, *Madibane High School*

Steve: My brother left earlier because by then he was a prefect at Madibane High School, and he was a member of the South African Student's Movement (SASM). So we never actually had our assembly, although we did congregate around the assembly. Instead of the principal coming to give assembly, it was my brother and two of his friends, who addressed the students.

That's when they said: 'We had a meeting on Sunday with the SASM executive, and we've taken a decision that we are marching to Orlando Stadium, so effectively there is no school today. Immediately when we disperse from here we are going to Orlando Stadium.'

But we decided to go via the central place in Diepkloof, because that would have taken us onto the road that leads to Orlando. We were hoping that somewhere along the way we'd be joined by many students,

46

because that's a busy road. That's a road that most students travelling to different parts of Soweto would have been on, trying to catch buses and taxis to their respective schools. We were hoping that as they were waiting for their transport, they would then join the march.

It hardly lasted for ten minutes; within ten minutes we had dispersed.

DINGANE LEBELE, *Madibane High School*

Q: On that day, was school normal in Diepkloof? Did you go to the assembly?

Dingane: Yes, there was normal schooling. But word was spread by students from other schools about the unrest that had broken out. So on the next day we followed. We started burning beer halls, post offices and we were shouting, 'Power!'

Q: Was there any particular reason why you joined?

Dingane: Yes. Some students had been shot and killed. Not only Hector Peterson. There were other victims.

Q: When you left school on the 16th, what did you see?

Dingane: Nothing. There were no soldiers in camouflage uniform. There were no riot police.

SOLOMON MARIKELE, *Rhulane Senior Primary School*

Q: Did you attend the morning assembly?

Solomon: In the early morning when we reached school, things were very normal for us because we were still students. We were not aware what is going to happen, but by twelve o'clock, eleven o'clock, they came at school, they said: 'Hey, no more education, we have to change the system, then we will learn again.'

Q: Who came to your school?

Solomon: I can say the comrades. Nobody wanted to identify or to tell you the original name because there was danger during those days. Once you can say, I'm who ... who ... who ... they came to your place and they harass your family and you can get killed.

Q: Did they come to your classes?

Solomon: They disrupt classes, they don't listen to teachers, principals, whatever. They tell us students: 'Hey, go home.'

They were just coming quiet. Sometimes they decided to come four or five. They were not coming in high numbers.

Q: Did the principal and teachers try to stop them?

Solomon: They tried, but they overpowered them, because even we the students, we supported the struggle. So they ended up co-operating with us.

Q: Who said that you must go home?

Solomon: Those comrades which were not at school at the time.

VICTOR KUBAYI, *Tiakeni Junior Primary School*

Victor: So when I arrived [at] school, we heard from other people that things were not going well outside. The principal decides now, the students should go out from school, because it seems as if there was policemen and soldiers all over our area. Those people were using tear-gas to disperse each and every individual. So there was havoc everywhere. Chaos everywhere. So we went [out] of school, then on the way there were those cars, Hippos [military vehicles], all over our area.

With June 16, the thing was organised, but it seems there were certain leaders who were leading everything. So as I was still young, the parents advised us to stay at home. There was shooting everywhere. So because of that thing, the following day we never go to school. It continued like that and then I don't remember very well, maybe it lasted how many days after that period.

MUZIKAYISE NTULI, *St Matthews School*

Q: Tell me about June 16th, 1976, from the time you woke up getting ready for school.

Muzikayise: June 16 was a normal day in the morning, but [the] afternoon is where we see there were some changes. There was some chaos around the country, but now at my school the gates were locked. We couldn't go outside to buy from the shops because everything was inside the schoolyard. There were spazas there. Sisters and fathers and teachers at the school organised that there must be spazas. While at that time we never used the word 'spaza', but we used [to] buy right inside the yard of the school. It was a strict school.

Q: What was the normal procedure at your school?

48

Muzikayise: We started with the assembly, praying and singing, then get to the classes, then we start with our subjects. Yes, just like other days, but [the] afternoon is where something different is happening.

While we were starting in our classes we could hear noises outside and there was chaos. We would have to get out of our classes to see what was happening outside. Only to find out – now they tell us [it] is the Black Power.

Q: Was the chaos also happening inside your schoolyard?

Muzikayise: At that time it was outside the schoolyard. There were those students from the high schools. They entered into our school to tell us that now we will have to stop learning because now is Black Power, because of this introduction of Afrikaans in Geography, History and Science.

Q: As your gates were always locked, how did the senior students get into your school?

Muzikayise: We contacted the principal, Sister Joseph, that there are students who want to enter [and] who want to have a word with you. They came in to our schoolyard.

Well, since she was a white person, I could see that she already knew what was happening, because they do have phones in their office and all that. You see, the equipment. So they do hear that something is happening here in Soweto. She welcomes that.

When [the students] went to the schoolyard, they told our principal that there are students who have died already, who have been killed by the police. At that time I did know it was Hector Peterson that was shot. The students were very angry. They say that we will have to leave school and go home because now is Black Power.

I was fifteen years old and I was doing Standard Six (Grade Eight) in 1976. I was about to write [the] June exam.

THAILANE NGOBENI, *Nghungunyane Junior Secondary School*

Q: Did you attend assembly on the 16th?

Thailane: On that day everything happened – we were prepared. We were going to school but we knew that there was something that was going to happen. So when we arrived there it was said that we continue, that was the first day.

Q: Did you attend assembly at all on June 16th?

Thailane: There was no assembly, everything was messed up. Even our principal, Tlakula, had realised that there is something. Immediately when we started during parade time – okay, I am a soldier now. It was not a parade but it was assembly. There we would pray, sing, we pray and we move to our classes and started with our schooling. But that day everything was dancing, some were wearing their clothes they wear at home, some were in school uniform. I myself was wearing school clothes, I was wearing a black, yellow and blue tie, that represents Nghungunyane.

We then proceeded as I've already mentioned until we were disappointed at Phutalushaka. We continued, even the Tsietsis were in our company by then, they did what they did, but we knew what we were fighting for. Imagine, our parents had no time to think, because of … liquor. Lounges and bottle stores and bars.

Q: How was the day from when you woke up in the morning?

Thailane: That was normal like all the other days. That day it came automatically because we did not start on June 16th. This thing was planned and when they came to fetch me, there were underground channels and we knew … knew that there are brothers. For instance, Mandela was in prison, some other guys were in prison, our leaders at the moment. Some of them are still living, some of them have fallen down.

So they recruited us.

We told them: 'Okay, come for us, we will do it.'

Those who are cowards refused. We thought that our aim must go forward because we were introduced to the slogan, 'Aluta continua', and when I ask what is 'Aluta continua', they say, 'Struggle continues'.

TULU MHLANGA, *Tiakeni Junior Primary School*

Tulu: [On] June 16 what I can remember is we were in the classroom when brothers and sisters came. They were carrying placards. I can't remember who was my teacher of that day but soon after she read the placards she said to us: 'Do you see that your brothers are toyi-toying? They are striking against Afrikaans.'

Q: Do you remember anything that was written on those placards?

50

Tulu: The placards – since we were inside the classroom we could not read [them]. The only person who managed to read them is our mistress who explained to us that they are striking against Afrikaans. The explanation she gave to us was that everything was going to be done in Afrikaans. For example, Maths was to be done in Afrikaans, so that is the reason why they disagree.

Q: When the brothers and sisters came, were they quiet or singing?

Tulu: They were singing and they did not enter into our school. They were passing and I am sure they were coming from Nghungunyane because they were from a certain street coming directly from Nghungunyane. They passed next to our school and that time they were going to Vuwani. Soon after that our school had to knock off. Actually our school knocked off immediately after we felt tear-gas, smelling [it] while inside the classroom.

There is a certain brother I used to know. His surname is Sambo. I saw him jumping the fence into our schoolyard as he was running away from the police. He entered our school and hid himself while the police were busy chasing him.

SOLLY MPSHE, *Morris Isaacson High School*

Q: How did the students approach your school?

Solly: I cannot tell you exactly what happened, because I was in the classroom. Everybody was learning. What I can tell you for sure was that there was no negotiations, because if there was any negotiations we would have expected to be formally addressed [and told] that is what is happening, and this is the reason why you must join the other guys, and surely that could have been done by the principal or by the teachers. These guys just came in and went: 'Out, out, out, out, out' and 'Amandla!' We didn't have something like that before. So it was firstly just confusion and later you realise that, hey, in fact, there was some hesitation. I remember just before going over the bridge, some of us were thinking of diverting to do our own thing, because the whole thing ... it didn't mean anything to us.

Some of us were fortunate in the sense that my father used to buy me papers daily [like] *The World*. I used to read and I knew there were problems at one higher primary in Orlando West where Afrikaans was in

51

force as a medium of instruction. So I could tie it up. Honestly I didn't understand why [we] should be forced to march. And I didn't even understand where we were going. I didn't grasp the objective of the march.

But the guys from Naledi High ensured that no one stayed [at school], because I remember we were trying to stay here. They ensured that we march. The control was there. I think they were making sure that we go in numbers. Yes, there were those leaders who were leading us and what later became known as marshals.

PHYDIAN MATSEPE, *Orlando High School*

Phydian: I was not politically conscious. We were busy with our mid-year exams. On the 16th we were writing a Maths paper. Unsuspectingly we went into the exam room; but while we were there we heard a lot of noise and shouting outside. While we were writing, one guy came. He is now well-known, Simon Majakathata Mokoena. He stood at the assembly stoep and shouted: 'If you don't join us, you are against us.'

When we went outside we saw a lot of schoolchildren, marching and carrying placards: 'Away with Afrikaans', 'To hell with Afrikaans', and we joined them.

Q: So Majakathata was a student at Orlando High then?

Phydian: Yes, he was a student at our school. We learnt that he was a member of the Student's Representative Council. He was in the same group with Tsietsi Mashinini and Kgotso Seatlholo.

Q: What time was it, when all this happened?

Phydian: It was around ten thirty a.m.

1. 2001: The Esso Garage on Old Potchefstroom Road in Chiawelo features in many of the recollections of the 1976 uprising as it was the site where students regularly stopped cars belonging to government agencies or private companies. Within a few days of 16 June, 143 vehicles, among them 50 police vans, were damaged, looted or set alight in the greater Soweto complex. Photo: Themba Maseko

2. 2001: On 16 June students from the far western townships of Soweto travelled by train to Phefeni Station in Orlando West in order to join with the young marchers from central Soweto who were coming along Mahalafele Road through Dube. From here they had planned to proceed to Orlando Stadium down Khumalo and Vilikazi Street past Phefeni Junior Secondary School. They were however stopped at the intersection at Uncle Tom's Hall and never reached the stadium. Photo: Themba Maseko

3. 2001: The Diepkloof beer hall which was burnt down during the uprising and never rebuilt, stood at the main intersection in the centre of Diepkloof. In later years a large squatter settlement developed on the land around the ruins. Beer halls and drinking places were specifically targeted. From the recollections of the eyewitnesses recorded in this book it appears that the aims were both looting and to rid the community of the evils of drink. Photo: Themba Maseko

4. 2001: Crossroads in White City, also known as Jabavu, is still a major intersection which links various parts of Soweto. It was the scene of various tumultuous clashes in 1976 as a number of political funerals took place at churches in the vicinity. Today a busy taxi rank operates from next to an informal market. Photo: Themba Maseko

5. 2001: In the late 1960s and early 1970s Uncle Tom's Hall in Orlando West was used for community functions such as boxing tournaments and the performance of plays. It was not used for political gatherings, but it was here on Khumalo Street that police met and confronted hundreds of students marching to Orlando Stadium. Photo: Themba Maseko

CILLIE COMMISSION
VOLUME II, pages 2-6

WEDNESDAY, 16 JUNE 1976
West Rand: Soweto

08h00: Scholars carrying placards gathered at the Naledi High School.
Tebello Motapanyane addressed them and outlined the route they were to
follow to the Orlando Sports Grounds. The vice-principal tried to address
the scholars but was driven off. Motapanyane led the march to Orlando
West past the Thomas Mofolo Secondary School and the Morris Isaacson High
School. Scholars from the Tladi, Moletsane and Molapo Secondary Schools
also arrived and took part in the protest march. The Morris Isaacson High
School was deserted, however. At the Sizwe Stores, scholars from other
schools joined the march.

   Scholars from the Morris Isaacson High School arrived at the Thesele
Secondary School in White City, carrying placards. The school principal
was driven off and the Thesele scholars followed the other scholars. Some
of the marchers forced motorists to give the Black Power salute. Already
at this stage motorists were being threatened with assault or damage to
their vehicles if they did not give the salute.

08h10: Mr D.D. Smit, an Inspector of the Department of Bantu Education,
travelling by car to Jabulani, drove past the Orlando West, Dube and
Belle Schools in the direction of the Morris Isaacson High School. In
Maputu Street, before the intersection with the Old Roodepoort Road,
marching pupils from the school attacked him in his car; he sustained
only minor injuries.

   Col. J.J. Gerber, Division Inspector for Soweto, left for Naledi to
investigate conditions in the area. He saw between 800 and 1 000 scholars
marching in the streets and reported to Brig. Le Roux that the scholars
were marching to Orlando, that motor vehicles were being attacked, that
the police were being pelted with stones and their vehicles damaged. Col.
Gerber stated that on his arrival at the Jabulani Police Station he found
that there were too few policemen to disperse the group of scholars.

08h20: A further 600 scholars fell in with the 900 scholars marching from
Naledi to Orlando. The marchers appeared to be in an aggressive mood and

55

gave the Black Power salute to police vehicles. Some marchers were wearing the Naledi School uniforms.

08h30: A crowd of scholars congregated at Sizwe Stores; among them were pupils from Morris Isaacson High School. Two reporters from a local newspaper fell in with the marching pupils. On their way to the Orlando West High School, marchers sang 'Nkosi Sikelel' iAfrika' and 'Morena Boloka Afrika' among other songs and carried placards. As the marchers made their way through Dube, their ranks were continually swelled by other scholars. An inciter of about 26 years of age was noticed in the group. This group later fell in with another group outside the Orlando West High School grounds.

A large group of scholars was seen in Mofolo Village near the golf course. Col. Kleingeld sent out three patrols, one to each of the three high schools in Orlando, to ascertain whether meetings were being held there. The patrols returning from Orlando West and Diepkloof High Schools reported that all was quiet. The third patrol reported that west of the railway line a mob of youths was on the march from the north, moving in the direction of the Orlando West High School. Col. Kleingeld investigated and followed the protest march by car, accompanied by two sergeants. The march comprised scholars and others. The moment the marchers spotted the police, they pelted them with stones. The scholars looked aggressive. Col. Kleingeld feared for his and the sergeants' lives and vehicles, and turned back to get reinforcements.

Col. Kleingeld requested reinforcements and issued revolvers and pistols to his men. With 48 policemen, 40 of whom were Black, he went past the Orlando Stadium to Uncle Tom's Hall, where scholars had gathered. He tried to address them. He was notified by radio that more marchers were approaching from the direction of Jabulani and Moroka. Stones were hurled at the police, and according to Col. Kleingeld the situation was highly explosive. The police used tear-gas to disperse the crowd. The crowd moved to Khumalo Street. An inciter, brandishing a knobkierie, danced at the head of the scholars. A dog unit joined the group of policemen. Col. Kleingeld ordered that the marchers be followed by Sgt. Hattingh, whom he joined later.

At this stage, Brig. Le Roux realised that the situation was explosive. He had too few men – between 300 and 350 – at his disposal to control the situation.

09h15: A Black journalist and a White woman journalist from the same daily paper arrived at the Phefeni Junior Secondary School and were warned by the local Black teachers to leave the area because of the approach of the Naledi scholars from the west. The White woman journalist was threatened by the scholars and left the area.

09h30: On his arrival at the Orlando Police Station, a White newspaper reporter was greeted by Blacks giving the Black Power salute. He could sense that the atmosphere was tense.

10h00: When the police arrived at the Tshabalala Garage, they were pelted with stones by about 600 scholars and their vehicle was damaged. Tear-gas had no effect on the rioters. A further 600 youths fell in with the first group here. The police were withdrawn because there were too few of them to take further action.

Chapter 4
Leaving school: the marches

BONGANI MNGUNI, *photographer*

Q: Why do you say it started with a dog?

Bongani: [The police] were on standby next to Paul Verryn's church. Just around there. Standby with dogs and watching the situation. They were not many – about twelve or less. Everything was sort of calm, everything was smooth, kids were up and down talking to each other, inside the school. Not a very big crowd. [The police] were not chasing them away, telling them to go back to school. They were just watching, but they were very close to the kids. Maybe at some stage, they were intimidating the kids. And that is why it happened. The joke was [that] some of the dogs would bark, hawu, hawu, hawu, when these [kids] were getting closer, and the kids run away. And then that was it.

[Some schoolchildren were] inside Phuti School, inside the schoolyard at Phuti. Phuti is a school next door to Orlando West High. There was nothing like a fight or anything. It is just that kids were gathering together, up and down the street, things like that. It was peaceful.

[A police dog] kept chasing the kids until they went inside the yard of the school. And then immediately they went in, they turned and then the others just grouped against the dog. The kids started stoning this dog. Some with knives were stabbing the dog. They kicked the dog, they stabbed the dog, stoned the dog, until the dog was dead.

But, soon, immediately after the dog, then everything started, and there was fire all over. And there was tear-gas all over. That is why I say it started with a dog.

Of course, the owner of the dog who was holding the dog, keeps running, following the dog, and because of the crowd he could not go through. But, in a second when he saw the dog, the dog was already dead and everything started. And [the police] started being like furious, you know, shooting whatever, and trying to tell the others that, hey we have a problem, now the dog is already dead.

You could see that [the policeman] is really, really, really angry. Ja, he was white, a white policeman. He was furious. I don't think he was scared. Or maybe [the police] took this thing very lightly – these are kids, we can handle them. Until kids started killing the dog. Probably it is then they saw that this is a big thing, it means business.

I never saw something like that before. And I was not expecting that to happen, I was just expecting a march to Orlando Stadium, a peaceful march. Even though on my own, I thought these kids are mad. You see, they want to march about this thing of Afrikaans. I didn't know that that was a very big thing . I just took [it] like hey, [it] is one of those things kids do for the first time, they want to march, you know, we will see.

I am a dog lover. I groom dogs. But seeing police with dogs I don't feel very good. They are just taking advantage of these poor animals to do their dirty jobs. I like dogs, I like animals, police I don't think use them rightfully.

DAN MOYANE, *Morris Isaacson High School*

Dan: We were singing and it was jovial, the mood, exciting, and with the placards we started going, we started going. We went and went. We passed Mofolo, other people were joining us as we were going along, other kids, and everybody was in school uniform, everyone. You looked around from left to right, people were in their various school uniforms.
Q: Was there tension at that stage?
Dan: There was no tension. There was that anticipation, that sense of ... Wow! You know positively, what is going to happen? We were all going to Orlando Stadium, and there we will publicly endorse a memorandum that will then be delivered by our leaders, who had organised this, to the government, [saying] that we don't want to be taught in Afrikaans in

school. Or at least we need to have a choice, because they were making it compulsory that we be taught in Afrikaans. We don't mind learning Afrikaans as a language, but it is against international convention. I mean, where else are you going to go with an Afrikaans degree?

Anyway we were nicely going and there was nothing, nothing tense in that sense, tension as in: 'Jees, I wonder what's going to happen.'

It was a sense of anticipation of what are we going to do. So we went and went, we got to Phefeni, by Maponya, when you go down there towards Uncle Tom's, we were coming there and we stopped, the whole thing just stopped. I was like 600 metres away from the front, from the right, and there were some of us who walked out, and journalists were there. I remember ... Nzima ... what's that photographer's name? Sam, ja, Sam Nzima. He took that picture of Hector Peterson.

He was there with his car and his camera, he was just chatting. So we walked out, I remember walking closer and closer because Tsietsi said he wanted to address us, and then people were moving in a circle so you could feel more people, and there was a tractor ... what do you call them, earthmovers, ja, those orange ones used by the municipal people.

He stood on top of it, and I was not far myself from that.

He said: 'Listen, police are further down the road, they have closed [the road]. They say we don't have permission for the march and they won't allow us to pass. We told them we want to go and just hand in the memorandum at Orlando Stadium, the others are coming there and we're going to meet.'

In the meantime people from Naledi and Emdeni are busy jollying from the back, so he is getting people who are singing and shouting as he is talking. And so they were saying: 'We want to go, we want to go!'

And then the police were just behind him, and they were coming closer.

There's a street that was coming from the houses, the other kids were there coming from Orlando West, so it was just packed around the side streets, from the main streets. And then I don't know what happened, because I didn't see it. He came down, and then we were there, and people saying, 'Hey, hey, hey,' and then suddenly there was this gunshot.

This gunshot suddenly, and we were down. I was 600 metres from there and people were running from that road and they were coming that way and they were saying that the police are shooting at us, I don't know what happened, and we just picked up stones. And I've never seen so many stones coming. It was a huge crowd – those police could not stand there, they would have been killed. By then Hector had been shot, and the news filtered that there was a kid who had been shot.

Q: Was Hector the only person shot that day at that particular time?

Dan: At that moment Hector was the only person who was fatally shot. There were other people who were injured from jumping fences and stuff like that, but at that moment, from what I recall, we heard of nobody else that had been shot. But other people had been injured and whether it was from the bullets or not ... There was a lot of shooting that happened at that time after the first shot was fired, because [the police] were stoned, they could not have [lasted] for longer because they could have been killed.

Q: Hector was thirteen. Was it a stray bullet or was it just an un-aimed shot?

Dan: I don't know if it was stray, because he was shot in one of the side streets, coming towards the main road. [I don't know] whether it was directed at him as a person or it was a bullet that these boers were shooting. I think there must have been a shot or two up, whatever, but the rest were shots into the crowd. The crowds were on the left, on the right and in the middle, and the stones came, and then the police retreated, they went, they ran further down.

Then the next it was: 'Hey, hey, they shot a child, they have shot and killed some kid.'

So it was a humming thing, that there's one child who has been shot. Then people were saying let's go back because the police are down there and then all hell broke loose.

Q: Those from as far as Diepkloof knew nothing of this?

Dan: They had not heard, we didn't know what was happening that side, I did not know what was happening – unless somebody had phoned. If Tsietsi and the others went into a house and they phoned, I don't know, but that side we did not know, and looking that side it was nice and quiet. I remember very well. We all went backwards now, and then at the municipality [offices] at Mofolo, Dube, things just went out of control. That whole day the fire by the municipal offices started, and beer halls started, and then helicopters came. Tear-gas, I smelled tear-gas for the first time on that day.

SOLLY MPSHE, *Morris Isaacson High School*

Solly: I cannot recall what was supposed to be the destination. But I just joined the march. I know that after five minutes I was also carrying a placard! We moved down over a bridge [to] Molapo and to Molapo Secondary. I'm not sure by the time we reached Molapo if they were in the classroom or if they have been taken care of by other high schools, because it looked like the plan was that the whole thing started at high school level. [The] South African Student's Movement was predominantly at high schools [rather] than secondary schools. I think by the time we reached Molapo they were gone.

And there was another school – what was that school in Mapetla? It has a Sotho name? If you go down to Mapetla East to Protea, to Moroka police station, it was a temporary, like the building was in plastic or what we call asbestos. But it is no more there. And then from Molapo, we went down Mofolo, well it was obvious [that] the students from Morris were already ahead of us. And we went down Morris to Mofolo Park, via Dube and up to where Hector Peterson Square is right now. And that's where we combined with all the students from all over Soweto.

Q: Were they singing?

Solly: No, the first time there were no songs. Let me put it blatantly to you: during those years we didn't know much, even the songs that we knew [in] those days would be like songs that we got by some chance from an LP, from the exile singers. You find that maybe out of 36 only five people knew the songs which were relevant. The songs started playing later on after June 16th, making people organised. The only song that you could have called political [in] those days was 'Nkosi Sikelel' iAfrika'. But to answer your question, we were just marching and the only [thing] that was happening there was the chant of 'Amandla awethu' – 'Power to the people!' Ja, no, no songs.

Q: What happened after you met as different schools?

Solly: When we arrived at Hector Peterson Square we heard that several people have been shot already, and one was killed, which turned out to be Hector Peterson. And there was tension like we did not expect: to be shot at number one, and two, the police had already barricaded the main road leading to Orlando East. In other words there was no way that we could have proceeded if we wanted to. They were a safe distance away from us but the message was clear that if we try to go beyond [a] certain point, they were going to shoot.

There was a state of uncertainty most of the time. We were just moving around, not knowing where to go. And there was no direction, like what are we going to do, in terms of this is the situation, let's call this a failure, or we made our statement, let's go back and tomorrow let's go back to classes. So basically what happened thereafter was a free for all, because it started with commercial vehicles who happened to be in the neighbourhood and people started stoning those cars and taking whatever is inside.

And even there ... there was no order formally telling us to disperse. People started moving out of that area. And if they came across anything that could be associated with the system, [it] was targeted. That afternoon I learnt the popular word: 'the system'. So, on our way back, anything that was associated with 'the system' was stoned and we managed to put our hands on anything to take home. Ja, that is the picture that I have.

Q: Which standing properties were damaged on the 16th?

Solly: Before we left that area, there was no indication that Soweto is going to burn. We were still disciplined, law-abiding kids. We just wanted to freelance, all right. And even the stoning was done by a handful of silly kids. It later turned to be a free for all. So, some of us were a bit silly, threw stones and looted. I remember the first vehicle that I came into contact with was a little van with spirits and brandy. The next thing is two nips in my pocket when I was running away from the scene.

DIKELEDI MOTSWENE, *Ithute Junior Secondary School*

Dikeledi: Now those other people came into our school, we were all together and started flocking to another direction.

I was holding Nthabiseng, as I said, and running.

I said to Nthabiseng: 'Let's go home. We don't have to go with these people. We don't know where are they going.'

She said: 'No, let's go with them.'

I said: 'No, I'm not going there, I'm afraid.'

She said: 'How are you going to go home?'

I said: 'The way I did come here! Who's going to tell me not to go home?'

Then we went like we were going home, and these other students were just taking us back again. Then [things] started to be a big snake, snake, snake, snake … oooh, it was terrible, when I remember that day. I don't know what was the time by then, because now the whole school was out in their classes, and these little ones also, they were out, we were just mixed, everybody. Some, they were taking the children outside, these small ones. The teachers think that maybe they mustn't go to this crowd, but there was this other group that was just going to take them out of their classes and tell them to run. They'd tell you to run, and you'd say: 'Run where?'

Some didn't ask, but they are running. You just see people running, and you run too. It was terrible. I wasn't in front, I didn't know who was in front. There were leaders.

People were singing. They were singing these songs, different songs, so many songs. Some of them we didn't know. Sotho songs. We didn't know what was going on, they were just singing the songs and we didn't know the songs. These leaders, they did know the songs, they were just chanting. Some of the songs were like wedding songs, if you know the songs, you'll just join them. I can't remember some of those songs.

They didn't stop. I remember, when I was just running with those people, we see another house there. By the time this group now, they are so many. We see police. I don't know if we were in Orlando by then, I don't remember exactly. We saw the police, the vans of the police. Me and Nthabiseng, we were just holding ourselves so that nobody was going to break us. We were just fastened to ourselves.

Then we just go out, we go outside of them.

I said to Nthabiseng: 'Let's go in this yard. Let's go in, maybe they will open for us if there is somebody there. We'll just go in and hide ourselves. I'm tired.'

Then we go there, and unfortunately that gate was locked. We had to go to another one, fortunately it was open. We go into the toilet – the toilets of Soweto, they are outside – we go inside to the toilet, we hide ourselves there. I think we stayed there about two hours.

We could hear the noise outside, when we are there! Singing, and now the hooters of the cars, and the shooting now. Yes, we could hear the shooting now. Now we are shivering, and we were crying. We were crying, and me and Nthabiseng, we were really crying.

We closed that toilet, and I said to Nthabiseng: 'We mustn't cry loudly, because they will take us from here. This will be a secret.'

Now we hear that the shooting goes down and down, you see, with the crowds. It's like a distance.

We say maybe we can go out now. Maybe if we don't go out now, the person of the house will think that we want to do crime there. We must go. We went out, you know, peeping to see if there's anyone who can see us. We were shocked!

It was smoke all over now, we don't know what's going on.

It wasn't quiet. It wasn't quiet. There were a couple of people around. They were just moving around, towards a place.

Now I was afraid to go home alone to my place, because I'm staying there alone with my little sister. Now my problem is my sister. How did she come back? Is she still alive? She was twelve. I was fourteen.

And I said: 'You know what, let's go to your home,' because Nthabiseng wasn't far from my place, where I stayed.

By the time we were moving to her place, we can see some of the cars are burning, and now we don't know what is going on, some of the shops are closed. And, remember we'd only had breakfast, we are hungry.

Somebody was hurt here on the cheek, there's the blood running here on the cheek, and he was crying. It was a boy. He was cut on the cheek. I don't know, it was like a scar, but there was blood coming out. We went to Nthabiseng's home. When we arrived at Nthabiseng's home, Nthabiseng has lost the key, and her mother is at work. So now we had to stay again, because when we reached there we also heard another sound of burning, bah!

I said: 'You know what, let's stay another ten minutes here. Maybe when we go out it will be gone.'

She said: 'What must we do?'

I said: 'Let's go and see if my sister is back.'

We went there, and she's not there.

KEDI MOTSAU, *Naledi High School*

Kedi: I can't remember [the route]! There were some primary schools that we went to, it was from our school, to Moletsane High School, then to Molapo and then we ran straight through to Orlando. When we arrived there, at Orlando West, everything had already happened. We couldn't even go through, because when we arrived at our destination, all the killings were already done, so we didn't know actually what happened.

People were okay, everything was going all right. They were excited. Ja, and happy. They were excited, but not ... I would not say they were happy, because they wanted to know what's going to happen.

Q: On your march, did you ever come across the police or tear-gas?

Kedi: Nothing, until we arrived where this guy was shot. Hector Peterson. No, I didn't see him, because there was lots of people – can you imagine the whole of Soweto's children? Unfortunately, we were not coming from one school, there were other schools that were near to that place, so they were already there. Naledi is the very far end of Soweto, so we were the last people to come over to that place. That's why we didn't see anything. [The body] was still there, lying there, but we really couldn't see anything.

When the police came, we had to go back, because everything was loose. The cars were burning and there were lots of police, police dogs, then came the tear-gas, and we had to move back, but we didn't know how to move back, because these police were all over in the trains, so you keep on moving, but you don't know where you are going to.

So we had to walk, and then along the way. We were [scared], because we didn't know how to go. Are we going to manage to go back home safely? That's our problem.

We were hiding. In the houses, when you see the police, you hide in the house and then creep back when it's clear. That's how we managed to get back.

Q: And were you affected by the tear-gas at all?

Kedi: It burns you. It burns your eyes, it's horrible.

I was with my friend Mina. She was fine. We were not hurt at all. You know it's not everybody who gets hurt. [But] we lose [our friends]! We lost them, and then we had to find out from them the next day: 'How did you manage to go home?'

Q: What were the streets like?

Kedi: They were full of people. They were running, some were hiding, running away from these police, because they were coming just behind us. I'm not sure whether [the police] would have shot at us, or whether they would have just thrown the tear-gas. Just for us to disperse. After the whole thing happened, the shooting of Hector Peterson, the students became excited and they wanted to fight back, and the only thing they could fight back with was stones.

VICTOR BUTHELEZI, *Lilydale Senior Primary School*

Victor: School was not normal and then we saw the police coming and they started firing tear-gas at us. We did not know what it was and we only realised when our eyes started itching.

Q: How did that happen?

Victor: There was no violence, only peaceful protest. We had already started learning in Afrikaans.

Q: How did the students organise at your school?

Victor: They went to the principal, Nkabinde. I don't know what they spoke to him about, but we were told to go home early. We were happy to go home early, but realised that something was wrong as bakery delivery vans were stoned and there was chaos.

Q: Was there anybody you saw being shot on the 16th?

Victor: There was, but I am not sure whether they died. I can remember someone who was shot by rubber bullets. His name was Bheki Solomon Mabaso. I can't remember in detail what happened, but I remember that delivery cars were looted in those days.

SAM KHOZA, *Ibhongo Junior Secondary School*

Sam: The first time we heard of it was during the short break. Our leaders informed the principal that students from Morris Isaacson were marching. We then joined one of the groups and marched to Orlando Stadium. There were different groups marching to Orlando Stadium, from different parts of Soweto.

Q: Did you reach Orlando Stadium?

Sam: Some did, and some did not, because on our way, police fired shots at us, and we were also tear-gassed. So the crowd dispersed.

Q: At what point did the police stop you?

Sam: At Orlando Power Park, near Vista University. They just arrested us. Before [that] they said we must stop marching, and go back to our classes. But we refused, we said we wanted to go to Orlando Stadium to ask the government to change this Afrikaans, to make it English. After that they tear-gassed us.

Q: What role did you play during the struggle?

Sam: We went looting the bottle stores. The first one was the one in Chiawelo – the one which is near the cemetery. Unfortunately at the time I was a non-smoker and non-drinker. Because we took the beers and the spirits, [and] dig holes in our yards. We were told that the National Party will come with machines to find out where are the beers and where are the spirits. My neighbour was shot at random three days after Hector Peterson, while we were looting. He was shot dead.

MUZIKAYISE NTULI, *St Matthews School*

Q: What time did everything happen?

Muzikayise: It was past twelve, past twelve to one. Sister Joseph allowed us to go home, because now it was chaos around. So when we went home we could see that now cars were burning, especially the company cars, those from town, those owned by whites, they are the ones who have been targeted, even the business, business people or the business of South Africa. June 16th was a day when we, the black people, rise their voice [against] the illegitimate government of that time, [the] National Party.

THOMAS NTULI, *Nghungunyane Junior Secondary School*

Thomas: Within the gate we saw a van parking, chasing this Chinese and all that, they called it fah-fee [an illegal betting game], in our language. So it's where things started. We ran to that van, we threw stones. So that van ran away. From there we were heading to another school, Vuwani. From Vuwani we went to Sekano-Ntoane organising all the students. We said: 'Pens down, books down.'

Then we went to Morris Isaacson. Nobody is going to write Afrikaans. We never needed Afrikaans, that was the issue.

It happened somewhere along the way. We met people who are working for the municipality, there was a boer and a black person. So that boer was attacked, they burn the car and that boer was killed by a mob. We were still young, we never understood what was happening. From there, there came the police. They started shooting with these rubber bullets, but they were not exactly using rubber bullets. They were even using the real bullets. We were tear-gassed and all that. Hector Peterson became the victim, first kid to be killed in that incident. Because we were all on rampage, that was 1976.

Q: You ended up reaching Morris Isaacson?

Thomas: Ja, it's after we left Morris Isaacson where things happened. You [don't] know exactly what things happened there. The police did disturb us. They were trying to calm us down, then we became angry.

Q: How was their approach?

Thomas: Their approach wasn't a good approach, because they started shooting and we were unarmed. We were just students, what we had [were] only pens. So we retaliated and we ended up throwing stones back to them, but they were shooting.

Q: Can you remember where the police blocked you?

Thomas: It was after Morris Isaacson that they blocked us. You know, I was fifteen, I cannot recall what exactly happened, when we attached that white person [who] was working for the municipality.

Q: Where were the police when you attacked this white man? Was it after the police had confronted you or before?

Thomas: It was after the police were busy with us. They were disturbing us. Some group went that side, some group rushed to the other street, so there was not order. Now we were fighting the police. Then came that white person. We said, he's also an Afrikaner ... We took it as if those are the people forcing us to learn their language by force, so he was attacked. It was racist now, racism, you get what I mean? Ja, it was racism now [that] we resorted to.

Q: Where were you when the white man was attacked?

Thomas: I was next to the situation. It was my first time to see blood, and I was so young. I was a toddler then. There were people older [than me], they did turn the car, burnt it, you know, I was scared. I was a kid, I was scared.

Q: From there where did you go?

Thomas: Now, thinking, back home and all the ways were blocked by police. They were shooting, arresting. Now I was running for survival, running for my dear life, the situation was changed. My eyes were, you know, full of tears, tear-gassed. I could see it was now survival of the fittest.

Q: Did you know tear-gas?

Thomas: It was my first time. I didn't know it. I thought it was one of the chemicals we used in the laboratory. Oh, it was not tear-gas, [it was] something they call a sneezing gas. It was like when you enter a house full of smoke. I was running for survival in order to reach home. So imagine, from Central Western Jabavu coming back to Chiawelo. I was so confused. You know, when you're running, [you] can't remember the right direction, jumping a fence, getting to a certain house. I mean they were using sjamboks and also we were sjambokked there. It was brutal. Running, I lost one of my shoes.

GEORGE BALOYI, *Nghungunyane Junior Secondary School*

George: We all joined. We went up through Dube Road and then entered Potchefstroom [Road]. Then we joined those who went to fetch those at Ibhongo and Sekano-Ntoane and Senaoane [Junior Secondary School]. Then we met at Potchefstroom [Road].

Q: Was it different groups?

George: Yes, we went out and it was ordered that some others should go here, and some others should go there. Therefore we went down straight and met at Regina Mundi. We walked through Potchefstroom [Road]. There were new leaders now. There was a lot of singing then. We did not know the songs, we were hearing them for the first time. [The songs] were okay, hey they were okay, because we were also fighting for those things.

Q: Did you know what you were going to do?

George: We were going to the meeting. We did reach [Regina Mundi], but when we came back, we came back very badly. We [were] tear-gassed for the first time. Well, the tear-gas was not bad, because you just felt your eyes itching. We just thought it was a mess. Smoke. But when we felt our eyes itching, we realised that it was tear-gas.

It started just here at Regina Mundi, because we were lashed by sjamboks and the dogs. The police gave us a warning and said: 'Ons gee julle drie minute.'

Q: Three minutes for what?

George: To disperse. Yes, then we said to them: 'Fok, fok, julle gee ons drie minute, fok, weg is julle.' (Fuck, fuck, you give us three minutes, fuck, get the hell out of here.)

They started with their things and we picked up stones and started to throw at them. And you know that it was our only gun, the stones. It was our bomb.

From Regina Mundi, I entered via Dhlamini. I was alone. I ended up crossing Potchefstroom [Road] then I entered that side of Chiawelo. From there I came back home.

Q: How was the situation in Chiawelo?

George: Hey, it was upside down ... it was havoc. Ja, something new had happened. There was no car which was allowed to pass by here.

Q: On arrival at home, what happened?

George: I stayed inside, but I did not end up there. I ended up going out, it was nice outside. The vice [looting] had started.

Q: Where did you do a lot of stoning and looting?

George: I was [stoning vehicles] at Esso Garage. Well, we used to beat cars. You come with a company car, we would beat [it].

Q: How did you recognise company cars?

George: It isn't that they are distinguishable. [When] they came wearing company overalls, you could easily see that this is the company car. Those [cars] of a black person are known. Immediately when we saw a dead, old car we realised that, okay, this belongs to a black person.

Well, we only stoned the cars and they would run. Maybe even [stone] the driver ... we broke the windows. We did not take anything and we did not burn them. No, we did not go for burning.

Q: Was it after you went to Regina Mundi?

George: When we came back home, I saw them coming carrying beers. They said that it is in Senaoane and then we went there.

Q: Where were the police by then?

George: In fact they were also afraid. Who can stand for a stone? We found that [the police] had not yet arrived. [There] was not only school-children, it was all mixed up. There was a loafer, thug ... all of us there.

ERICK NGOBENI, *Nghungunyane Junior Secondary School*

Erick: Those [students] who came to talk to the principal and request that the school must be off, they were also those who went with us outside the schoolyard and we started toyi-toying. Then, after that, I ran home where I took off my school clothes. Thereafter I accompanied my friends and followed those who were toyi-toying along the street. We went and got them where we joined their group and started singing with them again, walking along the road. I didn't know any of the group members. It was like I was seeing these faces for the first time.

While we were going, we reached the Senaoane bottle store, where I found that it was burning. I also entered and started to take liquor. I for one came out with liquor cans. When I arrived home, my uncle demanded that since I was young, I should give the cans to him. Because if the police could get me carrying these cans, they would shoot me, thinking that I am from the war which was taking place on that day.

The police had not yet arrived [at the bottle store] at that time. They arrived after we had taken liquor [and] the bottle store was already burnt down.

Q: What route did you use to the bottle store?

Erick: If I can remember well, I used the mochayineng street [row of Chinese shops]. Then I went down to Moroka police station. From there, I followed Koma Road. I doubled up at Vista, [at] Vista I walked to that bottle store.

Q: How was the situation on your way back from the police station?

Erick: The police that day, hey, along the way we met them. Some were running for cover. There are some places where we found that they shot something called tear-gas.

Q: Were you familiar with tear-gas?

Erick: It was the first day to taste it. I didn't know that it was tear-gas. As you know, we grew up without knowing that such things are used. I first thought that it might be a light mist that happened to occur just along the road. It surprised me, because it troubled my eyes a little, you see, even my nose. We were breathing in an unusual way.

Q: What time did your school knock off that day?

Erick: It was somewhere around the second period after short break. Our first break was at ten o'clock. For short break we had ten minutes.

72

It was not only schoolchildren who were busy running along the streets. Even in the bottle store which I have just mentioned, there were some elder people. I saw mothers and fathers. I saw them carrying cases of beers which were in the very same bottle store which I saw burning.

After I reached home and my uncle having taken that beer, I never stayed for a long time at home. I quickly got out and ran to the street to rejoin the others where the toyi-toying was taking place. The people that I ran to join were walking on Potchefstroom Road, they were moving towards Regina Mundi at Rockville, that is the street I remember walking on.

Q: When you were at Regina Mundi, what were you doing?

Erick: We started barricading and stoning cars identified as targets. By targets we were referring to Afrikaners' cars, company cars and municipality cars. Some were burnt.

JOYCE MAKHUBELE, *Tiakeni Junior Primary School*

Joyce: I went through the small gate next to the toilets [at the school]. Then to the street behind the school to Mange Street and went home. When I got out of the gate, I saw the police giving chase to certain boys. They were shooting with their guns. Then we also ran home. When I reached home, I explained what was happening to my mother. Suddenly my father came from work and said he was coming to alert us about what was happening. He also warned us not to get out of the house. He worked at Phiri Hall and also at the other places where they patrolled with the municipal vans.

We stayed inside the house but we sometimes went to peep through where we saw some cars hit, stoned and some burnt. The place where we witnessed the fighting was the Esso Garage. Cars were passing by and people [were] hit ... Clenched fists and when hooting cars passed they shouted 'Black Power!' Cars were hit by stones, but I for one never went to Esso. I only heard that, being just here at home. We used to double up to our opposite neighbour to watch. It was frightening to me. I used to peep through, but when I saw some [people] stoning cars, and that they [the police] shot, I ran and came back here at home.

STEVE LEBELO, *Madibane High School*

Steve: I think the idea of the route came about on Wednesday morning, on June 16th. Students at Morris Isaacson School decided that our destination is Orlando, and how do we get there, and they got around to the road, and as they marched along they were joined by hundreds of other students along the way. In Diepkloof we went around a kind of route that when I think back, I realise that it probably wasn't as planned as it should have been. We went to a central spot. We moved from Madibane High School and went to a place that is almost the centre of Diepkloof. That's where you have the biggest bus and taxi rank and there was also the beer hall and the post office. We were hoping [to meet] all the students from other junior secondary schools, because we were the only senior secondary school in Diepkloof at the time. There was Bopa-Senatla High School, which at the time was only four years old, that they would meet us. There was another school very close to Madibane High School, which was also a junior secondary school. Those, because they were very close to us, we simply joined together, as we moved out of the gates, and moved on to this central place, where we were hoping to meet up with students from Duplasina (Diepdale) High School. So there wasn't a kind of a plan into deciding the route of the march. From the assembly, we were heading towards the gate. By ten past, quarter past eight, we were already moving out of the school premises.

Q: What did the teachers and the headmaster do?

Steve: Well, I think what they had in mind was that this was going to be a flash-in-the-pan kind of thing, that it was going to last for an hour or two, and then, even if these students do not come back today, they will come back the next day, and school will be back to normal. The principal was Mehlape, Ntila Mehlape, who was very strict. When I think about it, I just wonder why Mehlape allowed us to have that assembly as we had it on the 16th June. Apparently, he must have realised that there was no point in trying to stop it, they were determined to have the meeting and to tell the students what was planned for the day. They just stood there and waited, and thought that maybe in an hour or two things will be back to normal.

So we left the school premises, and the principal and the staff actually remained in the schoolyard, and we were joined immediately at the gate by students from another school who were just across the road from Madibane High School. We marched on to the central place, at the crossroads.

A couple of things happened. By the time we got there, we started chanting and singing, and this is a central place and the students are coming in from all directions, into this place. We understood that we were going to have to wait a while, until hundreds of students had actually congregated there. But that in itself was a disruption, because there were young kids going to lower primary schools, who were drawn to this thing. So we couldn't actually move immediately.

I think we were there for the better part of an hour, maybe more than half an hour, thirty to forty-five minutes. The crowd had actually grown.

Q: And the little children, what did you do with them?

Steve: They were just bystanders at some point, but then other people came in, unemployed people who were in the township, youths who were not going to school, started joining the group and we suddenly had quite a huge group. We hadn't even started marching along ... what's that road? ... Africa Road, you know that takes you to Orlando, when suddenly news filtered that there were problems between students and the police in other parts of Soweto, and I think people started to panic a little. But something happened in Diepkloof that really concentrated the attention or focused the attention of the police. A couple of young guys who were not students, but who were perhaps unemployed, young adults, decided to attack the beer hall. All hell broke loose, and we hadn't even started on our march, when these guys attacked the beer hall, and people started throwing stones, and that's when the free for all started. Shortly thereafter, the post office was attacked, this was the central place, where you had all these things in place. Just behind the beer hall you had the administrative offices which were also attacked, but yet another group of students felt that what we needed to do was to go on in the march. They marched on to the central administration offices which were in Zone One. That was quite a big march, most of the students were in that one.

It was well after nine o'clock, it was past nine, going for ten when that march actually happened. Before I could get there, there were hundreds of students in front of me, and we were marching to the central administrative block in Zone One. That also went up in flames, and it was burnt down. People were killed, they were attacked, not physically, they were told to get out, and that's when I realised that this thing somehow has gotten out of hand.

That's the reason why the place was also attacked. This is where you had trucks, vans, cars belonging to the municipality, they were actually parked there. This was where Diepkloof was actually run from. So that place was also attacked, but these attacks were severe. Maybe one block might have been gutted by fire, and it would have been put out immediately, but that place was actually burnt down. In fact it was actually burnt down much later, this was part of the arson [and] sabotage that came later, but it was attacked initially in the morning, something happened, but it wasn't something very big.

I think anyone will tell you in Diepkloof that at around ten o'clock in the morning, there wasn't any kind of organisation. People were going in all directions. [At] just about the same time, the beer hall was attacked for the second time, and this time, it was a much bigger group that went for the beer hall, and it was just completely destroyed. People went inside, and came out carrying cases of beer and liquor, and that's when the police came in. I remember they sent in a chopper, a helicopter, and the police started shooting from the helicopter. This one guy who lived in Diepkloof, his name was Majas – I knew him personally, because I used to play soccer with him – unfortunately, he was the one who was shot in the head, and he sprawled there and he died on the scene. It was pretty gruesome. In itself it instilled a lot of fear in people who were not far from the scene. I think that that's when a lot of people started to head for home, and that's when they realised that the whole thing had turned serious.

What is interesting is that some students from Madibane High School had decided that the destination was Orlando, so they went to Orlando, but it wasn't in a well-organised march. Students were fleeing and some of them just decided [to go] to Orlando, and they came back late in the afternoon, around three or four, to give us information as to what happened outside of Diepkloof.

Q: After your friend was shot, did you carry on going to Orlando?

Steve: No, I'm not one of those who went to Orlando. Me and a couple of my friends decided we'd had enough, and that was around half past ten, eleven, so we went to a friend's place and saw it as a school holiday. We hung around there for nearly the whole day, until three or four in the afternoon. It was the nearest house we could have gone to. At that point, from ten o'clock, right down past one to two, it was pretty dangerous in the streets.

GANDHI MALUNGANE, *Nghungunyane Junior Secondary School*

Q: So where did you go when you left school?

Gandhi: From there we had to move up, you know my school, it's situated next to Dhlamini. If you don't know that place well, you won't be able to say whether that school is in Dhlamini or Chiawelo. So, there is a big street which is dividing Chiawelo and Dhlamini. There's my school, here's Dhlamini, and we had to follow this street. I think it must be Makhado. So we went straight up, and then there is a garage, it was Esso Garage then. Today it's [still] known as Esso, even though it's changed into Zennex. I think it's one of the first garages around there.

My father's house is not far from there. So now, seeing a group of students, everyone looked at that. People came out to watch the students, what they doing, where they going, because it was unusual.

We were there and we were singing. You know there is this song, it can be heard today, I can't get it out of my mind. They call that 'kubi' ... It means, 'It's bad, it's bad, even if they can shoot us, we've got bazookas. We are just going forward, no matter how bad it might be.'

And those songs, they were new to people like myself. When you are hearing a song for the first time, then it's exciting you, putting you somewhere. That singing – you feel inspired. The music inspired you.

My brother spotted me, and he had to call me. Calling me, when I went there he said to me: 'Where are you going? You can't go there. Just go home.'

I was so disappointed. He took me home, I was so disappointed. I had to stay there, I went to the gate, stood there by the gate, watching. So, some students were coming from different directions to run for cover, and I can't tell you what happened in the other schools.

And then I saw some others coming. By then my brother had left, he'd gone with his friends, he was going to town or whatever. So I found this as an opportunity. I saw these guys coming, there were roughly seven or eight. Then I had to join them. Joining them, running straight up, then following the street to Merafe [hostel].

It's amazing, you know, the number, we were trying to run for cover, and we never knew each other then, it was a joining, you see. I'm sorry to say we were running for cover! The group, they left us behind.

We were trying to catch up. We were busy running, immediately jumping Potchefstroom Road. At Phiri there is a place where we used to pay rent, the whole of Soweto used to pay rent in Phiri. We used to meet there. There were so many people, you could go there at six o'clock until six o'clock. So it's obvious to the whole of Soweto. It's next to Lizobuya House. It was unbelievable! From eight, we were more than five hundred. Everyone joined, you know.

I want to just tell you about what happened in Phiri. When we arrived at Phiri, here are these leaders now, from the group that grew up. They stopped us: 'Wait, wait, wait, we've got to turn this direction.'

It was still in the morning, because that thing with my brother stopping me, it didn't last. It didn't last even fifteen minutes, immediately when he took me home, he just said 'no'. And he never told my mother there were these things, this, this and this. My mother was expecting [the birth of] my younger brother. Can you believe, coming from the march and finding a younger brother? So, he never told anyone that Gandhi was doing this and this and this. He just took me home, and when he left I joined this group.

At Phiri, [there were] these guys who happened to be leaders, and of course they were leaders because they knew what was happening, unlike me. You know, I was just following, but they seemed to be having a direction, because they said: 'Wait, wait, everyone.'

We stopped singing and then they told us: 'No, we are using these directions.'

My knowledge of Soweto was just only Phiri. There was this thing that made us not to know other locations, because there was this thing of the Shangaan, the Venda. We were always victimised, like for example I could only go as far as Merafe [hostel] because immediately when they see me they say, 'Here is this Shangaan,' and then they beat us, so that's why I never had a clear knowledge of the other locations. I knew schools only. So, I was getting lost now in Phiri. We took the right direction, right-hand side, next to the hall, and we went on, and I was lost. I didn't know where was this place. But immediately when we get Koma Road, it's when I started to know, because it's next to Elkah Stadium, next to the Merafe station. Then I started to say, 'Okay, I'm here.'

Q: And how long did you stop there for?

Gandhi: Less than five minutes, just like, 'Wait, wait, stop, stop, we are taking this direction,' and then we followed. I was very excited about that, and I was eager to reach the place, to see the main event, to see what was going to happen there.

Q: How long did it take you to get there?

Gandhi: Soweto is a big place. It took us a long time. Imagine from Chiawelo, you don't go straight to Orlando Stadium. You go via Phiri, you know. We ended up being at Dube, it's like when we were busy moving, I sometimes got lost when we entered different locations. But when we go further, we'd get to a place and I'd know, this is the place. So when we reached Crossroads, I started to know, 'Oh! This is Crossroads.' And then we went to Dube station, and I knew Dube, because of soccer. And then from Dube, Orlando West too, now I was clear about everything there. I knew Orlando well, because of my soccer. Every weekend I used to go to the stadium, where we paid fifty cents, as schoolkids.

Q: What you were doing while you were marching?

Gandhi: Actually, there was nothing I was doing. You know, you're running, you're running and you're just following the rhythm of the songs. There was nothing I was doing, I was just running and enjoying that, sometimes some of us were falling and all those things.

Q: What did you see other people doing?

Gandhi: It was just singing and dancing. There were those who enjoyed that, in terms of emotions. You could see, this one is singing his heart out, unlike me, myself, who did not know a thing, sometimes I could just look at those who were singing their heart out, wondering as to why are they like this.

Some really knew what they were doing. Especially those who led the songs. Pains, you know, pains. It was like a person who was feeling a pain, and angry at the same time. You see they sung, and some of them, you can feel that this man knows what he is doing.

Q: Did you go to the Orlando Stadium?

Gandhi: We arrived [where] Mr Mandela's house [now stands], the one that was built immediately when he came from prison, it's in Orlando West. Down there, there is Orlando East, and Orlando West, so Orlando Stadium is in Orlando East. There is a train, a railway line which is dividing, and again there is a big road underneath there. So, Mr Mandela's house, it's just the last row of houses in Orlando West. We had to go via there, because we were rushing to get to Orlando Stadium. Some took the direction, there is a station called Mlamlankunzi, some took the direction, there is a bridge there, going the other way. The group I followed crossed the railway line, and surprisingly there was no one on the platform. You know, we knew how to cheat ... we sometimes open holes in these fences. Another thing I forgot to tell you ... I used to help my brother, he was selling peanuts on the track. Sometimes I used to help him. So, I actually followed the group that crossed the line, and then we entered the tunnel, there was a tunnel down there.

We entered the tunnel, not all of us. It's going to the side, the other side of the stadium. It leads to the other side of Orlando East. Immediately when you are there, you can see the stadium, the police station, all those things. So, some of them used the other road, they wanted to jump the fence to get to the stadium, because it was a long time from the tunnel to the stadium. It was difficult jumping for me, because even when I jump this side, I get a little bit hurt, you know, because I was young. I just followed those who were in the tunnel. So, there is this old age home at Orlando, immediately when we arrived there, everything went loose.

Firstly I saw people running. You can imagine, when you first see something, all the people running there. All the people running there. Then I heard shots, gunshots. I can't tell you whether they were bullets or what, but I heard shots. I started to run. We all started to run, before we can reach where things were happening, everyone was running. I started to run to the Orlando community hall, so I rushed to that place. I knew Orlando East because we had people like Jomo Sono [the soccer star] – everyone was dying to see where Jomo stays, I knew where Jomo stayed because early in the morning, early before the game started, we could go around showing everyone, 'This is where Jomo stays.'

Rushing to the community centre, I saw now a police Land Rover. They were using Land Rovers then. So I saw these other guys throwing stones at the Land Rover, really, I joined, I joined. I started now picking stones.

I had realised that the police were fighting us now, let me say us, because I was there. So now, I joined. I started to fight, throwing stones.

It's just next to the community centre. When you jump, there's a street there, they were jumping, running there, these guys who were throwing stones at the police. I picked up stones, throwing as well. Immediately now, when we started throwing stones, there was falling. I'd realised that there was another Land Rover coming through the dusty streets, another Land Rover was coming this side. Some were fighting police-men there, some here, it was a mess. So they came, this other Land Rover, then they started shooting at us. Tear-gas and stuff like that. You can imagine a gun sound, you start to smell something is bad there. I ran; I got my knee hurt, when I jumped a fence. When jumping the fence, I tore my trousers, and I fell. It was like everyone was running. Some guys were really bold, and they knew what they were doing, because they could run, throw stones, running maybe for cover, hiding themselves, take stones and going back again. I started to realise that the whole of Orlando was full of policemen and full of fighting.

Q: So what did you do?

Gandhi: I started to say I can't wait for this, because there was nothing **like** a friend next to you.

Q: You were alone?

Gandhi: Yes. I started to think about Chiawelo now. I ran. I was scared. It was bad the way things were happening. I was feeling like the police [were] killing everyone, although I never saw someone die. I just felt that I was going to be killed, everyone was going to be killed there. I started now to run away from it.

TULU MHLANGA, *Tiakeni Junior Primary School*

Q: Who were you with and which direction did you follow?

Tulu: Mostly they were those I was at school with, Ben and Solomon. Solomon entered his home as I proceeded home, where I took off my school uniform and followed the group. I joined the group which was

81

at Esso Garage and then went to Dhlamini Two. From there we went to Sekano-Ntoane. When we arrived there the bottle store was already burning. As the fire had just started we took beers out with us.

Q: The people around you were singing. Do you remember the songs or the lyrics?

Tulu: Songs like the one I liked most: 'Senzeni na' and 'Nkosi Sikelel' iAfrika'. They were new to me. They were troubling me spiritually, because I was starting to get the taste of politics. I immediately understood the message which they carried.

Q: Were you arrested for participating in the June '76 riots?

Tulu: I was arrested for stone throwing. I was arrested at Esso Garage and taken to Moroka police station where we were beaten by the police and released. I was arrested for the second [time] again at Esso Garage. This time the riots were a little calm and we saw two guys fighting. I still remember one guy's name. He was Victor. When they were busy fighting the police van came – we used to call the [municipal] police Black Jacks then. When we saw the police van we stopped concentrating on the fight and started stoning the van. While we were busy stoning, another van appeared at the back of the garage. I run past [my] home to a house next to Butiza's place where I found a woman who was drinking tea. I then pretended as if I was [also] drinking [tea]. When the police came in they took me for that family's innocent child. But when they left the house the woman said in Tsonga that I will cause her troubles from the police. Unfortunately the police had not gone far and one of them was a Tsonga, thus they came and arrested me. They dragged me before I could reach Bob's house. I was swollen, as I was repeatedly hit with the back of the gun.

As they were municipality police they took me to Dube Vocational [School] where we were ordered to do some hard exercises. They also ordered us to fight amongst ourselves. As we were five, they did punish me, but I refused to [be punished] and as a result I was further punished by the police claiming I was cheeky. We were released very late, at about six, and I then went to my relatives who stayed at Mofolo. They clapped [hit] us; they mostly used hands.

Q: In your opinion what made the police beat you and then just let you free?

Tulu: They realised that we were young and that we were just following our brothers in politics. Yes, they were frightening us. We were not asked any questions, we were just beaten and told that we were still young for what we were doing. We must not be misled by our brothers.

Q: Around Chiawelo where you participated, did you ever see someone shot?

Tulu: Here in Chiawelo I saw a person already injured but [I] never [saw] how he was shot. It was exactly on the 16th. Exactly on the 16th. Sometimes you found that the victim's head is swollen, but he was not hit by the [real] bullet, but a rubber bullet as they call it. Even the rubber bullets were found from the 17th.

PRISCILLA MSESENYANE, *St Matthews School*

Priscilla: But during [the day] further incidents of unrest broke out. We heard gunshots from the direction of Esso Garage and we rushed there to see what was happening. Trucks were stopped and looted, and police fired shots in an attempt to disperse the crowd. As the crowd scattered, my aunt was shot, but we could not stop to find out how she was. We were terrified as we ran home. [It was] early in the morning, about ten o'clock.

My aunt's name was Sylvia. She was at home. When unrest broke out, she also rushed out to see what was happening. We too went out of curiosity. I was eager to participate in the action.

I lived very close to Esso Garage where most of the action was. So I ran home and hid under a van parked in our yard. The boers came into the yard, carrying guns. They grabbed some of the people who ran into our yard. I stayed under the truck, quietly, until they left. I stayed there until I was certain they were gone. By the time I came out, I could smell tear-gas fumes in the air. I was terrified that the boers would beat me up like they did those they grabbed in our yard.

When I emerged from under the van, things had quietened down a bit. I quickly ran into the house where I locked myself in. Peeping through the windows, I could see police in armoured trucks chasing people and beating them up.

HENDRICK TSHABALALA, *Gazankulu Senior Primary School*

Q: Who told you to go home?

Hendrick: When the siren went on, we did not understand that maybe the school was out, or we were supposed to go home or we were going for a certain period or the following period. They sent one of the prefects who was on top of all the class prefects. We got off to the assembly, whilst outside the prefect told us: 'Get out! Get out, with your books!' Therefore we got out to meet at the assembly. Then the whole staff of teachers and mistresses and the principal with the vice came. The principal is the one who told us that: 'Today we knock off early. We won't tell you [what] is happening, you'll just go, now we are releasing you from here. Each and every child must go to his or her own yard at once.'

We left the way we used to go with my friends. We took the usual route home. On the way, we just saw them passing, proceeding to another Venda higher primary called Mambo. Ja, then people like us were staying near it. From there they went to a secondary [school] called Vuwani where they collected the elder students. Then we went and entered our respective yards. Without knowing what was happening we changed our clothes and took our soccer balls and went to the soccer grounds and started to play.

Q: Does that mean on June 16th 1976, Midway was quiet?

Hendrick: [Around] Midway [station], there was no problem. The only problem was the smoke which we felt while we were playing. We felt a very strange and tormenting smoke while we were playing. We were badly sneezing and that is the only and main reason that made us to part ways. There was no trouble. There was no problem. We just saw the helicopters flying all over without knowing that there was danger somewhere.

MUZIKAYISE NTULI, *St Matthews School*

Q: Did you encounter any problems on your way back home?

Muzikayise: Hey, at that time it was excitement ... well, excitement with fear. It was the first time to experience such thing, to confront, to burn cars, bottle stores. There was a bottle store next my school, not far from my school, in Rockville [which] was burning at that time. So people were drinking, but we could not take the liquor at that time because we would have to march home as youngsters. It was exciting; [but] at the same time you don't know what is going to happen the next hour.

Q: How was the situation along the way?

Muzikayise: It was havoc actually. When I mention havoc, I mean it was a destruction.

MARTHA MATTHEWS, *Kelekitso Junior Secondary School*

Q: What happened after meeting with your fellow students?

Martha: It was so shocking. At the time, as high school students, there was nothing like fear [or] of going back where we came from, that is home. We wanted to go and see what is going on, what is happening.

We went to Dube and then went to school. We were just scattering all over. It was confusion now. You did not know whether you are going or not, because we [were] already hearing news that in so-and-so place, so-and-so was injured. You know, you understand, radios were broadcasting.

Even my brother was arrested on that day of the 16th, because these boers followed us inside the houses [to] which we ran and tear-gassed us. At the end of the day when I arrived home I found that [my brother] was not there. So those who saw him being abducted by the boers came and told my parents that he was arrested and taken. So I can't remember well if he came back after two days or three, but it was so sad, more especially to my side.

Q: How was his condition?

Martha: He was injured, but he was afraid to go to hospital. It was frightening. I think at that time I was in Zone Three, there by the post office that was burnt. We were going to watch. The police were always with us, so we kept on running, we were always fleeing all the time. They were shooting with rubber bullets. They were shooting at random, they did not choose.

VUSI ZWANE, *Rhulane Senior Primary School*

Vusi: We walked through the road commonly known as Main Reef Road, but unfortunately we did not go a distance. Immediately when we reached White City we met the police contingent. They told us to disperse. So instead of dispersing, our leaders — who were the likes of

Murphy Morobe, Cyril Ramaphosa, Tsietsi Mashinini — addressed us and told us to calm down. And [someone whom] I think is now confined to a wheelchair — he was also a leader. As he was talking to us, the police decided the other way round. They fired tear-gas, the rubber bullets and real bullets at the same time. As a result we were forced to disperse.

Q: Tell me about the meeting.

Vusi: The addressing meeting was held at Elkah Stadium, everything started there. Our group was stopped by the police in White City. On that side of [what is now] Mshengu Tshabalala [squatter camp], by the garage on that way that goes to Mofolo. The one that joins Dube.

Q: What can you tell me about the groups?

Vusi: In fact we were all different schools. We were both leading to one direction. I mean, you know that when you are from the same school and you know each other, you automatically find yourself together. We were in different groups, but we were going to one destination. Everyone followed the people he knew. Some were ordered to go via Five Roses Bowl and we walked this side. But we were going to the same direction, because we were so many, you see.

Q: How did you meet with the other schools?

Vusi: When we left Nghungunyane, we collected students from Ibhongo and those of Senaoane Junior, coming from Dhlamini and Senaoane. We then went together down to Elkah Stadium. Some schools came from their direction and we all met at Elkah Stadium. I can just say that this march came from different angles, because some of the students were coming from as far as Naledi, as far as Moletsane, as far as Mapetla, Phiri, from the whole area. So the right centre was Elkah Stadium, because everyone knew Elkah Stadium. Also for the boers ... the boers must not know our meeting place.

Q: Do you remember the names of your SRC members?

Vusi: I am able to recall a few of them because we had Phindi and Aaron Dube who was my opposite neighbour, and Thailane who stays behind those shops and the other one called Chris. I understand that he is now late. He died in exile, he was a cripple. He stayed on that side of the station. There were others who stayed behind on that mountain [koppie]. They were so many.

Q: How did you come back home from White City?

Vusi: When the police fired at us with tear-gas and guns (remember we were not used to tear-gas – it was painful to our eyes) everyone had to run. Some ran into the houses anywhere. You'll find clothes and make it wet by water and cover your mouth and nose. Running was not easy because boers were all over. I became so surprised when I found out that some schoolchildren did not reach the point that we have reached. They decided to loot the mochayineng; it was a small centre [run and owned by the] Chinese. They used to sell furniture, butcheries, grocery stores and all those sort. That is where it was burnt. It is the same place at which [the soccer player] Ariel Pro Kgongoane was shot and killed. I never went to participate, because I was still young. I just ran straight home. Along the way, I was able to see everything that was happening. At the Esso Garage I found that roads were blocked so that the cars should not pass. It was just busy. I ran home.

Q: When did you decide to participate?

Vusi: My grandfather was released earlier at his workplace because it was already heard that there were troubles in Soweto. He found that I was not at home. My grandmother was so scared. She thought I am one of those kids who have been shot, because she already knew that there were schoolchildren who went to the march. On arrival I explained to them all what had happened where we came from. So I went home to change my school clothes and went back to Esso Garage to join those who were busy stoning cars.

Q: What inspired you to join?

Vusi: What made me to participate is that I saw this thing as something that affected the students. I can simply say all the students of Soweto because this thing started here. So, I had to identify myself with it, because I am also part and parcel of the students. I had to take part.

Q: How did you know the targets?

Vusi: Potchefstroom was targeted because it was the road which was used by cars driven by many people. From the Indians who stayed in Lenz who were doctors, and also white doctors who came from private clinics who stayed in town. We easily identified them through their colour. We identified government cars by the words written on them.

My biggest participation happened at Esso Garage, because it is nearer to my home. That is the place where we were blocking delivery cars. As you know, Potchefstroom is the biggest road in Soweto, so any cars that resembled company names in town, furniture stores, bakers, breweries, cars from Coca Cola, [were there]. That is where I participated the most until a certain lady died. She was behind me. This happened just at the back of Esso Garage. That is where I got frightened and realised that this can cost one's life.

Q: Did you completely stop from participating?

Vusi: Not completely, but it is where I started to realise that this thing was a serious issue now, that it can cause the death of a person. You know at first I took it [that] we throw stones at cars and [it] ended there. We never thought that somebody can die. You know, I was traumatised because it was my first time to see a person die ... especially losing her life in front of me. It traumatised me a lot.

Q: Was this lady a student?

Vusi: No, this lady was not a student. She was just an elderly lady who was just passing. She did not know what was happening. So because the boers were just shooting anyway, she was shot by a stray bullet. It was just a passing bullet. Maybe it could have got me simply because she was just behind me. It hit this lady. That is why I was so traumatised.

THAILANE NGOBENI, *Nghungunyane Junior Secondary School*

Q: From Nghungunyane, which direction did you take and follow?

Thailane: When we left Nghungunyane we assembled at Lwamondo Shop at Nghungunyane, [with] those guys we schooled with from primary to secondary. There was Camp, whose surname I forgot, and Norman Sunduza. Norman left Basani School and he joined the police force. Unfortunately when he came back the riots started – it was not actually the riots, but instead it was our rights! Sunduza came back at our school and fired a shot and we attacked him with stones. After that we went to this Venda school near the Star soccer grounds called Phutalushaka ... it is Vuwani or something like that.

We walked to Naledi – there was no extension at that time, it was just an open space. We were blocked. We were so many schoolchildren. We reached Orlando ... no, White City, and it is there that we were blocked. One Chinese survived, maar it was a certain white guy who was a superintendent or something like that, he was hit by a 'pik' (pick-axe) in front of our eyes. So who killed that [white] guy I don't know, it is not our business, therefore it was the beginning of the riots.

BAFANA HLATSWAYO, *Nonto Junior Primary School*

Q: Tell me about the events of mochayineng.

Bafana: We arrived at mochayineng ... I think it was past two. We went there in a big group. It was the nearest place which was not yet touched. Remember it belonged to the Chinese, that is why we called [the place] mochayineng. [The Chinese] were powerful, they had everything.

Well, we were running on the direction to mochayineng and when we finally got there we saw that the place was still intact so we started looting and burning the place. Everything happened so fast because as we [were] running to this place we were being chased by the police. I went into this grocery shop and I started taking things, anything. As I walked out next to the shop I was in, there was a butchery and that's where everybody was. They were taking all the meat from the refrigerator, it was such chaos that I didn't even want to go in. The danger was that the refrigerator door was closing and, locked inside, you can't come out. The other thing was that the place was now on fire and it was falling down on them.

I remember running like mad with others who made it out of the butchery, they had chunks of meat and they were running. Moses Zondi Buthelezi, my best friend, had a full sheep with him and we were running together. I had a big dish with lots of other things inside the dish and we were running, heading for home. Moses Buthelezi was a pillar, you know. Whenever I got tired he could pull me and ordered me to take cover, he was always next to me.

Lots of people were injured back there due to the stampede since everybody wanted their share of the meat. Most of them did not survive. I heard later that many people died there. Although I knew none of them, I felt sorry for them.

Q: Is Zondi still alive?

Bafana: Alive and kicking, and even now he was reminding me of all the things we used to do.

Q: Do you remember anyone shot at mochayineng?

Bafana: There was another accident, because I remember I was carrying a big dish. I was no more running towards the direction I came from. I was now running forward, because the boers were coming behind us. So I run towards the direction of Regina Mundi, because Regina Mundi was just near where we were at that moment, and still it was Old Potchefstroom Road.

I think there is a guy who was shot there. I realised after that [he] was a popular guy who played for a big [soccer] team in Soweto. He was also shot while I was busy running. I heard later that this guy was playing for Kaizer Chiefs. He was the star of Kaizer Chiefs, the late Eric Ariel Pro Kgongoane.

Q: What happened to the goods you looted?

Bafana: I took a dish and my friend was carrying meat. I remember, I run with those goods to Pimville, Kliptown Station until I reached home. So, at home they were so strict [about such things] that they gave me a beating and saying that I should take back those goods. They did not want those goods, but I don't know where [the goods] ended up. I don't remember taking them back, but I don't remember where they ended up.

PHYDIAN MATSEPE, *Orlando High School*

Q: Which direction did the marchers come from?

Phydian: North. Students from Selelekela which was a junior high school opposite Orlando High also joined the march.

Q: Did you know any of the songs that the marchers were chanting?

Phydian: No, I never knew any of the songs. The only song I knew was 'Senzeni na'. It's a hymn, so having grown up in church I knew it. By the time the group reached Orlando High, Hector Peterson was shot. We didn't know who he was then. We only learnt from the newspapers who he was.

Q: Did you join the march?

Phydian: We joined a large group. I recognised Tsietsi Mashinini. I knew him from church. He was a member of the Methodist Youth Club. So we were singing and chanting and soldiers came and we started running in all directions.

Q: So what happened next?

90

Phydian: The soldiers surrounded us and we threw stones at them. Then they started shooting, so we burnt the municipal offices and any building that belonged to the government – even cars. Unfortunately we ended up injuring innocent people.

Q: Which buildings were destroyed on the 16th?

Phydian: In Orlando the municipal office was burnt down. In Orlando East the rent office was burnt down. At the first office there was a fruit market which also fell under the municipality, it was also burnt down. I remember there were also shops that were burnt down because the owners refused to give us paraffin when we asked for it. We used paraffin to burn down these government buildings.

Top: 1976: An aerial photograph of Regina Mundi Catholic Church taken from the north. Buildings behind the church (in the foreground) had been set alight. George Baloyi recalls the key role of church in the uprising: 'It started just here at Regina Mundi, because we were lashed by sjamboks and the dogs. The police gave us a warning and said, "Ons gee julle drie minute."' (We give you three minutes.). Photo: *Rapport*

Bottom: 1976: In the area around Regina Mundi Catholic Church in Moroka municipal buses as well as commercial vans, lorries and cars sporting company logos were stopped, attacked, stoned and looted. The students knew that by bringing the traffic to a halt on Old Potchefstroom Road, a major artery to the west, they were causing major disruption. Photo: Bongani Mnguni

Top: 1976: As soon as widespread unrest erupted, the South African army was placed on alert and troops were deployed outside Soweto. Here an armed white policeman stands guard at a rather deserted entrance road to Soweto, the crowds seemingly keeping a safe distance. Photo: *Rapport*

Bottom: 1976: Most eyewitness reports of the 1976 uprising mention the omnipresence of the police in Soweto. 'Listen, police are further down the road, further down the road, they have closed, and they say we don't have permission for the march, the demonstration and they won't allow us to pass,' Dan Moyane recalls Tsietsi Mashinini telling them as they prepared to march. Photo: *City Press*

CILLIE COMMISSION
VOLUME II, pages 6-10

WEDNESDAY, 16 JUNE 1976
West Rand: Soweto

10h30: Several thousand students congregated round a stone-topped knoll
near the Orlando West High School. Witnessed testified that the crowd was
between 5 000 and 6 000 strong. From the evidence it seems that pupils
from, *inter alia*, the following schools took part in the rally: the Naledi
High School, Morris Isaacson High School, Orlando West High School,
Orlando North Junior Secondary School, Empangeni Higher Primary School,
Themba Sizwe Higher Primary School and the Thesele Junior Secondary
School. Col. Kleingeld's party was attacked with stones, making it impossible for him to address the crowd. The patrol consisted of approximately
four police motor vehicles, three heavy-duty vehicles and two patrol vans
carrying dogs. Four Black men were inciting the scholars. Those present
included adults and other youths not in school uniform. The tear-gas to
disperse the crowd was not effective. Only one tear-gas grenade went off.
A baton charge was also unsuccessful. The police were attacked on their
flanks and could be surrounded. Some of them were struck by stones. Col.
Kleingeld fired five pistol shots over the crowd, without effect. After
that he fired 20 shots with an automatic rifle in front of and over the
crowd. Other members of the police also fired shots with their revolvers
and pistols, although Col. Kleingeld had not given the order to fire. A
Black boy, H. Ndhlovu, who was inciting the crowd, was killed. Two police
dogs were killed and mutilated by the crowd. One of the dogs was doused
by petrol and set on fire. Police vehicles were damaged by stones. Hector
Pieterson (sic), a Black boy, was fatally wounded by the police. A woman
reporter took his body to the Phomolong Clinic. Maj. Viljoen and Col. van
Niekerk joined Col. Kleingeld. They proceeded to Moema Street. Sgt.
Hattingh's vehicle broke down and was stormed by the bystanders. Tear-gas
was subsequently used to free him. Col. Kleingeld again fired shots with
his automatic rifle. Col. Gerber, with three other vehicles, attempted to
join the group, but their way was barred by the people at the rear of
the crowd. They were immediately pelted with stones but managed to drive
through the crowd at speed. Col. Gerber ordered that the police withdraw

94

to the Orlando Bridge, where they took up position on open ground. The crowd of about 5 000 people came to a halt approximately 500 metres from the police.

Apparently, not all the scholars had arrived at the point where they had planned to gather. A witness who was at the Mapetla Garage at that stage saw scholars approach from the west and the south. Those he saw coming from the direction of Uncle Tom's Hall were apparently already beginning to move away from the Orlando West High School. In this particular area a large number of scholars and non-schoolgoing youths and adults were milling around everywhere. Some arrived in vehicles, singing and shouting, screaming and joining the crowed that had already gathered there.

10h45: A witness, Mrs S.A. Carruthers, and three of her White women friends had entered Soweto earlier that morning to deliver fresh vegetables to certain nursery schools. In the area in which they were, but which she cannot identify with any certainty, they did not see any rioting or hear any gunshots. At approximately a quarter to eleven they decided to return to Johannesburg. In a street, probably Khumalo Street, near the Orlando West High School, they found themselves amongst a crowd of rioters, consisting of scholars and adults, and were attacked with stones. The windows of the motor-car were smashed and all four of the occupants injured. Although the attackers rocked the car and tried to lift it, the driver succeeded in driving though the crowd, thanks to the physical protection given her by one of the passengers. They reached the Orlando Bridge, were escorted to the police station and taken to hospital.

10h55: A West Rand Administration Board (WRAB) official, Mr J.H.B. Esterhuizen, was driving along Khumalo Street when he was attacked by youths near the Phomolong Clinic. Pupils from the Morris Isaacson High School took part in the assault. Mr Esterhuizen leapt from his car but was surrounded by the youths and beaten to death in the alley opposite the clinic. Judging by the marks on his clothing and body, it would appear that they also tried to burn his body. Members of the police had driven up Khumalo Street, but did not see this incident, probably because of the chaos there. Mr Esterhuizen's body could be removed only about four hours later.

11h00: A Chinese driver of a Kombi was attacked by the rioters and in attempting to escape, he knocked down and seriously injured a young Black girl in Khumalo Street.

Two White men in a truck were attacked by stone-throwing rioters. They escaped to the Orlando Bridge and were not injured.

In the same area, a truck carrying liquor was attacked and the driver fled. The vehicle was then looted and the liquor distributed. The truck was set on fire.

Two policemen from Meadowlands were pelted with stones while they were carrying out an investigation at the Phefeni bottle store. One of them was slightly injured, and their vehicle was damaged.

11h10: A train driver reported that Black men had pelted his train with stones and that windows had been smashed. An officer and other members of the Railway Police investigated and reported that things were getting seriously out of hand. Trains were manned by policemen, and police protection was provided for the following places: Mzimhlope, Phomolong, Phefeni, Dube, Inkwezi, Inhlazane, Merafe and Naledi.

Tsietsi Mashinini addressed scholars arriving at the Morris Isaacson High School. He ordered them to stay away from school for the next two days; on the 20th further orders would be given. He assured them that both he and other leaders would see to it that Afrikaans would not be used as a medium of instruction at the high schools and announced that the police had shot dead two scholars and wounded eleven.

11h20: A large number of people – men, women and youths – were milling around the offices of the Youth Centre in Jabavu. They became excited and were shouting and dancing. In another part of Soweto, Orlando East, WRAB's new sheltered employment workshop was officially opened at eleven o'clock. This function was attended by *inter alia* the WRAB chairman Mr M. Mulder, the Chief Director Mr J.C. de Villiers and his Chief Welfare Officer, Dr L.M. Edelstein. During the proceedings, word reached them of the riots in the other areas and Dr Edelstein then left by car for the Youth Centre.

At about twelve o'clock he arrived at the centre. His motor-car had already been damaged by stones. He ran into his office and locked the door. A WRAB official, Mr R.E. Hobkirk, was trapped in another office in the centre. The stone attack on the building continued to grow in violence, and it was clear that some members of the crowd wanted to kill

at least the Whites in the building, if no one else. They eventually
forced their way into the building, battered down the door of Dr
Edelstein's office, attacked him and dragged him outside.

The attack abated briefly when tear-gas was used in the vicinity and
a helicopter flew over the building. Mr Hobkirk took this opportunity
to escape from the building. He noticed Dr Edelstein's body in the
entrance. In fact Dr Edelstein was either unconscious or feigning death.
He managed to rise, but his attackers dragged him outside, where they
eventually beat him to death. Shortly after one o'clock his mutilated
body was removed by helicopter. Mr Hobkirk, who had been hiding in the
Sizwe Stores nearby, was taken to safety. Two eighteen-year-old scholars,
K. Dhlamini and L.J. Matonkonyane, were charged with the murder of
Dr Edelstein. Their confessions implicated them, but, because a mistake
had been made in taking down their statements, the court ruled that their
confessions were inadmissible. Both were acquitted.

12h00: The police refused White reporters entry to the danger zone and
they had to obtain information and news from their Black colleagues.

12h15: In the course of the morning, a Black woman social worker from
the Department of Bantu Administration and Development paid an official
visit to parts of Soweto, accompanied by a White woman student. They did
not see any incidents until their motor vehicle was stopped by aggressive
youths on the Phefeni Bridge. The youths threatened to assault the woman
student. She was taken away by well-disposed pupils and placed in the
care of a clergyman. The police later removed her from the area.

12h30 to 13h00: A television newsman, who was accompanying the police on
patrols in Soweto, observed looting and arson by youths and adults at
this stage.

13h00: Bottle stores in the Phefeni and Dube areas were broken into,
looted and set on fire by various groups of Blacks. WRAB offices were also
set on fire. The police were pelted with stones. Tear-gas was used with
limited success.

The office of the station commander at Orlando was rigged out as an
operational office to co-ordinate police operations.

Chapter 5
Afternoon: lunch-time until after dark

STEVE LEBELO, *Madibane High School*

Q: What did you do on the afternoon of the 16th?

Steve: We decided to stay in that house. Some people were attacked in houses. Two people are walking down the street – when a police van emerges, they know they have to run. Whatever house they run into, the police will follow them into that house. I think that's when a lot of people were getting killed and injured, during the day, as this thing actually spread out to different parts of the township.

But, you know, we stayed put for the day. We were hoping that the next day it would be school as normal, but by six, seven in the evening, we realised that too many people had been killed, and that this thing had gotten out of hand, and it was clear that there was no way that we would be going back to school.

Then it spread to other parts of the Witwatersrand, and then it was a foregone conclusion that we can't go back to school.

Q: Your friend, Majas, who got shot: did you just leave him there? Did you have to go and tell his parents?

Steve: Someone did. We were in Zone Three at the time and this guy lived in Zone Four. Already we were beginning to sense that there was no way that we could cut across Zone Three to Zone Four, so we needed a house where we could hide. We stayed there until late in the afternoon, and then as we moved out, when things were beginning to cool off a little, we saw a lot of people who had been with us in the morning and we started to get a lot of reports.

A guy who lived across the road from my house, Gordon, went up to Orlando West, and he was in the crowd that was addressed by Tsietsi Mashinini. I heard that after Hector Peterson was shot, Tsietsi was able to address the students. What in fact happened was that the Johannesburg City Council was using tractors with trailers for collecting garbage, and one of these was driving past, soon after the incident, and it was attacked, it was overturned, and Tsietsi stood on top of it to address the students.

[He told them]: 'Our intention was to go to Orlando Stadium, and hold the mass meeting there, but since there has been these disruptions, it seems that we may have to disperse.'

Apparently a lot of things were happening, the whole thing had got out of control, and that's the report that I got from Gordon. But a lot of other people came back saying that they've seen so-and-so being followed by the police, being shot, getting injured, or some of them getting killed, and that's when we got to understand the enormity of the whole thing.

My brother came back late in the afternoon as well. He had been to Orlando High School, not to Orlando Stadium. There was no point in going there, the whole place was cordoned off by police, but there were students inside Orlando High School [whom] he met there, and I think that there were a couple who he knew from the South African Student's Movement. So they got together there, and started talking about what happened during the course of the day, and he came back home late in the afternoon.

Q: And when you left your friend's house that afternoon, what was it like outside?

Steve: Well, this was at about two o'clock, three o'clock in the afternoon. You would see police cars, police vans, perhaps going in the opposite direction, but you'd still be looking around, wanting to make sure. Whenever a car appeared, we were suspicious of it, we'd quickly go into a yard and hide. If you were walking around the main road, Magutso Drive, which is the main road in Zone Four, you'd still have to look over your shoulder and make sure that there isn't a car coming. From time to time you'd see a crowd of people dashing this way and that way, and you'd know that police are nearby. So it was that kind of cat and mouse game between police and students, for the rest of the day, until late at night.

When people returned home from work, [who] had already heard stories of what had happened in the township, some of them were expecting, you know, what they found: Soweto was up in flames and that students had not gone to school. There was a bit of stoning, but I don't think the targets here were the people coming back from work, because there wasn't a stay-away called for the 16th June, so people could not have been stoned because they went to work. I think the clashes were ongoing clashes between the people in the township and the police, as people returned from work. Some of them got hurt, with perhaps buckshot being fired at them, tear-gas, but there were not many fatalities on the night of the 16th June.

Before I forget: a white doctor was actually killed. Dr Edelstein. There were council offices in White City, and there was a Dr Edelstein, who was caught inside the council offices, next to which was the administrative offices. Having heard of Hector Peterson's killing, three young guys went into the offices, found Dr Edelstein, murdered him with an ice pick. I think that is one story that is worth following up. He was the first white victim of '76. Two of those three guys later stood trial, and were charged under section six of the Terrorism Act, and I think they were sentenced to long prison sentences. I don't know what ultimately happened to them.

GANDHI MALUNGANE, *Nghungunyane Junior Secondary School*

Gandhi: I started now to run away from it. I went straight to this Orlando Power Station, to join Potchefstroom Road. Vista of today was not there. So, I crossed the mountain [koppie] between Soweto College and Vista, then jumping that side. It was bad, because the police were all over, so with my trousers torn, I felt they would realise that this is one of the guys who are making trouble.

Q: Were you badly hurt?

Gandhi: Yes, yes, yes, it was bad, because I was just limping. So, crossing, I went straight to Pimville. Do you know why I know Pimville?

The new Pimville, it is full of these Shangaans, so Chiawelo and Pimville were the same people. So going to Pimville it was not dangerous
for us, we used to go there. As I said, it was Shangaans one side, Vendas
one side. So I went there, but it was difficult for me. When I arrived
in Pimville, I had no place to hide, because we had to go into the back
streets.

I never saw a policeman there, until I reached Kliptown, Kliptown
Station, then I went to Dhlamini. There was this problem of how am I
going to get home, with these trousers torn like this? Immediately, when
I reached Chiawelo, the events of Orlando were now all over Soweto.

Q: In the time it had taken you to run home, the situation had spread
and become worse?

Gandhi: Yes. Immediately when I arrived home, I realised that everyone was aware of this. I was with my sister – when I was doing Standard
Six (Grade Eight), she was doing Standard Seven (Grade Nine). She
didn't join this. She started now feeling bad for me because I was not
there.

There is one thing I want to tell you about the politics. I didn't know,
I was not politically aware by then, but there was this thing of knowing
about the bad treatment from the government. There were these 'Black
Jacks' people – they were part of the city council, council policemen,
who came to our houses, waking us up in the night, demanding a house
permit, checking there is no one who is there illegally. Brothers of mine,
they grew up in the Northern Province, and they'd come with two
wives. My mother is the owner of the house, it is registered to her. The
other mother, the other wife of my father, also lived in the Northern
Province, and she would often come [to visit].

So these 'Black Jacks', they used to come, every time, arresting some
of the family members there. So we were not on good terms with these
people. We didn't like them. If you failed to pay rent one day, they come.
So, I was aware of that, the way we got treated by the government.
Not by the government, I saw these people, these 'Black Jacks', as the
people who were ill-treating us, not the government. So immediately,
when I reached home, I went to a friend of mine called Victor. I went
to Victor's place, stayed there.

Q: How long did you stay there for?

101

Gandhi: About thirty minutes. Then, Victor's mother had to feel that: 'No, you are hurt,' and she went home to tell them I'm there. When I arrived home, my home, everything was loose, because that fighting was happening. Especially Senaoane. Chiawelo, it is a calm location, it is very calm. Senaoane, it's where everything was happening, this fighting now, these gunshots. But very soon, when I went to the house, there my sister was trying to boil water, trying to heal me, and the street next to my place, there was this fighting. There was tear-gas, it started.

I stayed inside, because I was hurt, but these others were going out to see what was happening. There was this other brother of mine, Charlie, he came running, complaining that there was something that was burning him. It was tear-gas. We never knew of tear-gas then.

My mother, in that time when I arrived home, had given birth to my younger brother. That same day. So there were these other people trying to help her. She was in the bedroom, I didn't realise until I saw that there was this baby here. This tear-gas started to overcome everyone. They said to my brother, 'Hey, you're lying, there's nothing like that.' Immediately the tear-gas started to penetrate the house, so it was a mess.

Q: And the new baby?

Gandhi: It was bad about him. They tried everything, to put him inside the wardrobe, and he was fuming with this tear-gas. You know, we are not allowed to go to hospital when my mother gave birth, or anyone gave birth. That day was bad, we tried to get into the bedroom for cover, thinking the tear-gas won't penetrate the bedroom. It's where we saw everything. When the sun set, I managed to get out, because I was feeling a little okay, to get water to put over our faces. It was when the police were shooting tear-gas haphazardly, you could see it, the whole of Chiawelo was full of smoke, full of this tear-gas.

We didn't sleep that day. We didn't sleep. It was bad. Late ... two or one, then the tear-gas was no more.

SOLOMON MARIKELE, *Rhulane Senior Primary School*

Q: What happened on the way from school?

Solomon: I just got home safely, but it was not the question of myself only. All the students were having the same problem. We fought against apartheid. You know, it was just something which is horrible.

102

DAN MOYANE, *Morris Isaacson High School*

Q: Did you partake in the beer hall looting?

Dan: Not the beer hall looting, but ja, the attack on the municipal offices. Everybody was doing it.

Q: Why did you attack the municipal office?

Dan: I don't know. Nobody said government is the target, nobody came to me and said that, but it just happened, mob psychology it just became. Maybe somebody in front said: 'Municipality, if the police kill you, attack the municipality.'

Maybe. I didn't hear that, me, personally, talking as an individual. When I got to White City, from there I went back, because I was walking back home. I said: 'Hell, no, I don't know what is happening.'

As I was heading back home, there was a group of guys who were saying: 'The police must pay, people were talking about this.'

Q: Was this one or two o'clock in the afternoon?

Dan: This was mid-afternoon. People are talking and there are stories now.

'Did you hear that some people got into Winnie's house at Phefeni?'

'So-and-so has been caught.'

Everybody is just talking.

'They've burned Number One office there by White City.'

And stuff like that.

I went [with] a group of guys. We jumped because then the offices were closed – most of the superintendents were whites, remember, they were white and they were gone. So we jumped in there, guys broke in the doors and everything else, and then petrol ... petrol was now freely available and petrol-bombing started, everything was burnt.

That office, I don't know how much of it burnt, because when I came back it was changed. But I remember being chased by helicopter. Down Crossroads, because our office was up there by Mama Lettie's in White City.

So we ran down with a group of guys and suddenly there was this helicopter, and they were firing tear-gas from a helicopter. We were just running from the police. We then went into Mulaudzi's place at the store. Mr Mulaudzi closed the store saying, 'You guys are naughty.' He knew my dad very well, he was a Venda man, said he would tell my father. He ran out, locked the place and he was gone. That was the end of the day, I can't remember what happened after, except to listen to the news.

I went home ... My sister was small, shame, Ellen was at primary. Ellen was born in 1968, so she was not even ten. She was eight and doing Standard One (Grade Three). I didn't say anything, my mother and father were talking: 'What did you guys do? Come back and tell me.'

My mother told me later in the evening that she was worried, she had heard about it in town that schoolchildren have started 'Black Power' in Soweto. She came back and she wanted to know about her son. I am sure every single parent that day wanted to know.

VICTOR BUTHELEZI, *Lilydale Senior Primary School*

Q: Were the soldiers inside the school premises?

Victor: The soldiers were moving all over the yard, but not inside the school. They [were] moving outside the yard and all over the location and all over the area we are residing at. What happened is that some of the eldest students from the high school did come and talk to the principal before. They advised the principal to take the children from the school.

Q: Was it by force or peaceful?

Victor: They didn't fight with the principal, but they advised him – because now all over Soweto, all the schools at that moment were out. The students were marching and joining, all happening in that day. They thought that if they would leave us at school, the situation was not good for education or for lessons. So they decided we must go back to our homes and then maybe as young students we can be safe.

Q: How was the situation on your way back home?

Victor: It was all over trouble. All the Hippos were moving in the area, so we were advised that when we go out the school we shouldn't group ourselves and go in numbers. Actually we were supposed to move [in groups of] maybe three people. The soldiers were moving all over the area. So [were] the Hippos because it was dangerous for everybody and we hid ourselves. When they pass we were running all over the area.

Q: How was the situation outside?

104

Victor: By peeping from the window [of our house] we could see people running, some other people falling. They were running all over, they even ran inside the yard. Those people were chasing everybody. They came in the street and sjambokked everybody, beating everybody whom they found in the street.

PHYDIAN MATSEPE, *Orlando High School*

Q: How did you get home?

Phydian: Getting home was very difficult because there were police all over, and we were not allowed to be in groups.

Q: When did you get home?

Phydian: Late, around five p.m.

Q: How did the parents react to all this?

Phydian: Most parents heard about it from the radio while they were at work, and they came home early. I remember when I got home my mom was already there, she came home earlier than usual. My parents were just happy to see me alive and well. Nothing was happening in Diepkloof then. Most students who lived in Diepkloof attended school, especially high school, in other parts of Soweto. But we had leaders in Diepkloof who organised these marches. Guys like Abe Lebelo, Steve's older brother, and Joy Rabotapi. On the night of June 16 1976, we were making petrol bombs and testing them.

Q: Were you not afraid for your life?

Phydian: As youngsters we didn't care much about that, especially after we lost some of our friends. That's why we used to refer to the stone as an African bomb.

SAM ZIKHALI, *Ibhongo Junior Secondary School*

Q: What can you tell me about the night of the 16th?

Sam: We were drinking, throwing stones. I joined the group – every group [was] moving down, up and down, and policemen were shooting. Some of the guys were injured, some were drunk. Right, right up until past twelve, one o'clock the following morning, it was the same thing.

We went to Orlando, dodging these policemen, throwing stones ... well, there was shooting, you know, and all these things. We were in close shave with death and at that age we didn't know that we can die and we didn't worry. It happened all just like that, right up to the 18th day, though I don't remember whether it was the 18th day and the school was closed.

They said: 'Nobody must attend, Ibhongo is closed.'

And so we stayed at home for three years, not attending school for three years.

THAILANE NGOBENI, *Nghungunyane Junior Secondary School*

Thailane: When we came in the evening of the 16th, we went to Chiawelo bottle store and burnt it. We then went to the beer hall where sorghum beer is sold [and] we burnt it. The police arrived with their Hippos. We did not want to see a Hippo.

Q: What about the night of June 16th?

Thailane: I did not sleep at home on that night. That was because of the petrol bomb [that] I designed on that mountain [koppie] on which there is a [water] tank. It was still open veld then, the place where the office stands today. I went to sleep in the shop. I stayed for three weeks and the police were searching for me.

Norman Sunduza is the one who was mostly searching for me. Norman Sunduza is still alive even today. He came to me to ask for forgiveness. I made my own TRC (Truth and Reconciliation Commission) and forgave him. He knows himself that he once pointed me with a gun. I remember when he told me that I will get you. We schooled together. Okay, we used to trouble him at school – he came to school with soccer balls and we took them. I think that is why he joined the old South African Police ... the old regime. While I was in Mozambique I wrote him a letter and told him that I will be back. Our post office was not as big as it is today, after receiving that letter they went to tell my parents.

Q: As you were sleeping at the shop, what was the situation outside?

Thailane: We heard dogs barking outside, and that was the sign. They were searching for me all over, the whole night of the 16th, but they never get hold me. I started my guerrilla warfare here in South Africa, inside Chiawelo, before I got trained, before I moved and went outside.

HENDRICK TSHABALALA, *Gazankulu Senior Primary School*

Q: What about the night of June 16th?

Hendrick: On the night of June 16th, no one slept. I heard gunshots, a lot of running. You never understood what to do then. You never understood what was going to happen then.

I was inside the house, people were running around the streets, even the police cars were running around.

Q: Were you peeping through the windows?

Hendrick: Peeping through ... you could not. How could you peep through while there were gunshots?

BAFANA HLATSWAYO, *Nonto Junior Primary School*

Q: At what time did you see trouble heading to your area?

Bafana: I started seeing these things at night, because all the people who used to come home early failed to do so. Even the elder people who used to take off their uniforms did not do likewise. That was a sign of danger.

We never understood what was going on. We were even forced to go to bed earlier. We heard that so-and-so place was burning. In the night [was when] we realised that something was happening somewhere.

MUZIKAYISE NTULI, *St Matthews School*

Muzikayise: My brother too, well, we ran during the night. We go to the hide-outs to hide ourselves, because now we could see that these government [people were] getting to some houses and certain houses were running away. The boers went there, shot them there in those houses.

June 16th was the start. The following day was worse.

I couldn't go straight home, because even myself I was drunk. I slept with my friends in the hide-out till the following day, so that our parents could not see that now we have already tasted liquor. We have been very young at that time to taste liquor; our parents were people who were very African culturally. Our parents could not stand that nonsense of seeing a young child drunk, roaming around. So your parents would give you a thorough beating, punishment, you know.

SOLLY MPSHE, *Morris Isaacson High School*

Q: How was the evening of the 16th in your vicinity?

Solly: It was just tense. Ja, it was quiet and tense.

Q: At [what became] Hector Peterson Square, were there some police?

107

Solly: Policemen were there. They had to put some barricades, just to make sure that no one proceed.

THOMAS NTULI, *Nghungunyane Junior Secondary School*
Thomas:During the night of the 16th, I was asleep, I heard noises, people: 'Heeee!'

Now I woke, I went outside, and stand by the gate. I saw some people carrying some liquor, looting the bottle stores. You know, it was a confusion and my brother came with his friends by that time. He took a bottle, making a petrol bomb [with] petrol. They couldn't even use matches, they were just pouring [the petrol onto] the flame of fire. They did that at home, that is why my brother was arrested.

They were burning councillors' houses and all that, attacking the people who were working for the government by that time. They said, 'This is our only weapon.'

Ja, drinking, bottle stores and all that looting, burning.

GEORGE BALOYI, *Nghungunyane Junior Secondary School*
Q: Tell me about the night of the 16th of June.
George: Eish, it was very nice. It was Christmas, we drank free beer.
Q: Where did you find the beer?
George: We went to fetch [the beer] at the bottle store. I helped myself here at Senaoane, in the street that leads to Skyline [shopping area].
Q: Were you already a liquor drinker then?
George: No, I did not know liquor. Some other people were dancing. Some others were busy drinking beer. At the other side we were busy stoning. The police came with Hippos. When we saw a Hippo we ran and they shoot while we were busy running. They tear-gassed and we picked up the tear-gas and poured it with water. We took Zambuk [ointment] and Vicks, and smeared on our eyes, and we went back there. When he shot, we threw a stone.
Q: Were you not afraid that you might be killed?
George: Well, you started to feel the fear when you were already at home: 'Because of that, I could have died.'

108

VICTOR BUTHELEZI, *Lilydale Senior Primary School*

Q: How was it when the evening approached?

Victor: It was very smoggy as there was a lot of tear-gas fumes. I was at home watching. I was very scared and when there was trouble I was the first one to run home. Our parents used to warn us as well that we will be hurt and shot if we went out. So we were scared and did not go out.

Q: Was your sister always at home?

Victor: Yes, but she would come and go. Sometimes she would be with her friends and I could hear them saying they were going to march or not wear uniforms to school.

MUZIKAYISE NTULI, *St Matthews School*

Muzikayise: It happened that [for] about maybe two hours or three hours or four hours the police came. When they came they started firing in rampage. There was a neighbour of mine who is in a wheelchair today, she was shot that day.

The very same day when now we are running away, we see the sister is lying down on a street there.

'Sister, what is it now?'

She said: 'I have been shot.'

Only to find that the bullet has penetrated through her stomach to her spinal cord, but she did not die.

Q: Was this on June 16th?

Muzikayise: Exactly the 16th of June, around nine in the evening.

Q: Did you try to help her?

Muzikayise: It was very bad because you can't help the sister, because the police were moving. In such a way that we are still speaking with the sister, the police came with the Land Rover and we had to run away, leave the sister lying there.

Q: How did you feel as you left her there?

Muzikayise: Well, at that time I [was] used to a white man. The whites in South Africa – we used to respect them as a youngster, I didn't know bad things about them. But at that time I could see that these people are very much dangerous. The elder brothers and sisters, those from the high schools, told us the meaning of Black Power, that now we have to retaliate.

109

VUSI ZWANE, *Rhulane Senior Primary School*

Q: Tell me about the night of the 16th.

Vusi: The 16th was one of those days I have never seen in the whole world because it was smoke all over. Then those old people who took advantage and went to work. Some were breaking in the bottle stores and stole liquor. Beers. It was noise all over, noise throughout the night. The police were also searching for people. They went around knocking ... and did all those things. They were just searching for boys, for any boy. That thing forced us to run away from our homes. We went to sleep in schools because they came to our homes searching for boys.

What in fact led us to sleep in the schools was because we heard that the police have started a house-to-house search. They started at Midway [station area]. So some of the guys managed to run away from Midway to this side. They told us: 'Guys, don't sleep at your homes, because the police are doing so-and-so.'

And we organised ourselves and took our blankets and entered the schools. We thought that they will never think we would sleep in the schools. And then we went to schools like Tiakeni. Some went to Nghungunyane, some went to Tshilidzi and so forth. We slept in the night in 1976.

Q: Were you not afraid that they might find you?

Vusi: We had the fear that they might follow in the schools. A person like myself was posted, that is to say, I was not supposed to sleep direct in the school. I must be somewhere in the corners. If I can see any sign of them, I must just run back to the school and tell them: 'Here they come.'

It means that I was used as an informer because I was young at that time.

110

1

2

3

4

1. 1976: Bystanders watch as smoke, possibly from a burning car, makes it almost impossible for drivers to see the road ahead. The arson and smoke caused great confusion. Dikeledi Motswene recalls: 'We can see some of the cars are burning, and now we don't know what is going on.' Photo: *City Press*

2. 1976: Soldiers in camouflage uniform gather at police vehicles at the side of the road, presumably having put up a roadblock on one of the roads leading into Soweto. Emotions running high, students could not resist stoning and even burning police vehicles. Photo: *City Press*

3. 1976: Within hours of the start of the initial peaceful and high-spirited march on 16 June, violent confrontation with the police was sparked off. One of many young men arrested by police officers with the assistance of the armed forces, is being escorted away, presumably to a police vehicle. Photo: *Rapport*

4. 1976: Bongani Mnguni, a freelance photographer at the time, took this photograph of a burning vehicle late at night at an unknown location somewhere in Soweto.

WEDNESDAY, 16 JUNE 1976

West Rand: Soweto

14h00: South African Police reinforcements arrived at intervals from the Johannesburg, Pretoria and West Rand Divisions.

According to observers, the disorderly conditions were exploited by tsotsis. Among some residents there was general drunkenness. Fewer children than adults took part in the looting.

A vehicle was stopped in the Phefeni area, the liquor it was carrying was seized and the vehicle was set on fire. The liquor was distributed among members of the public.

Maj. Viljoen came across a crowd of about 300 scholars and adults near the Morris Isaacson High School. They were aggressive and threatening, but they were dispersed.

Brig. Le Roux undertook an inspection flight by helicopter over Soweto, which seemed to be in chaos. People were gathering in several places. Vehicles as well as buildings were on fire, and parts of the area were under a pall of smoke.

A report was received at the Orlando Police Station that three doctors were trapped in Mofolo, and a vehicle was sent to their rescue.

14h30: The West Rand Administration Board (WRAB) bottle store at Phefeni was set on fire, as were WRAB offices and bottle stores in Orlando East.

15h00: The WRAB offices at Phefeni were set on fire by the same group that had destroyed the bottle store earlier on.

The WRAB offices at Diepkloof were set alight. When the police arrived, they encountered two groups of Blacks who began throwing stones. Two private vehicles had already burned out. Two Black men who were inciting the crowd were shot on the orders of a police officer.

The WRAB offices at Meadowlands were set on fire.

15h00-17h00: Arson and looting took place at the bottle stores at Nhlanzane, Moroka, Mofolo, Chiawelo, Senaoane, at the post office in

Molopo; at the library in White City; and at the clinic in Senaoane. The Mapetla Hostel was also set on fire. The windows of the Phiri Hall were smashed. The Etikeng and Vukani Schools were burnt down. Firearms were used by the South African Police in these incidents. Arrests were made and a number of looters were wounded.

Bottle stores at Zola and Moletsane in Jabulani were looted. The police used tear-gas and firearms. At Zola, seven persons were arrested.

15h30: Col. T.J. Swanepoel arrived in Soweto with three officers and 58 men as reinforcements. They divided into two task forces.

The task force under Col. Swanepoel came up against a crowd of between 4 000 and 5 000 Blacks at Uncle Tom's Hall in Orlando West. The crowd was overturning motor vehicles, starting fires and throwing stones. Warning shots were first fired, but thereafter shots were fired at the inciters in the group, after which the crowd dispersed. A Black man was hit. No bodies were found at this stage.

16h00: Major-General W.H. Kotze, Divisional Commissioner for the Witwatersrand, joined the Divisional Commissioner for Soweto to assist him in exercising control in the area until Monday 21 June 1976.

The crowds broke up into smaller groups, and vandalism was rife.

16h15: A Black man was shot dead by the police at the Mofolo Central Bottle Store.

16h30: The clinic and administrative offices in White City were set on fire, as were a number of motor vehicles.

17h00: About 40 Blacks tried to set fire to taxis in Jabavu. The crowd attacked the police with stones; shots were fired and two Blacks were hit. It was subsequently ascertained that a Black man, Mr K. Tokota, had died. An investigation revealed that about 20 vehicles had burnt out.

17h00-20h00: Arson was committed at the WRAB offices on Orlando East, Orlando and Dube; stone-throwing and looting occurred at the Dube Hostel, as well as four shops in the same complex; the bottle store in Orlando East was looted. Tear-gas and firearms were used in these cases. Arrests were made and a number of looters were wounded, but the wounded were sometimes removed by members of the public.

17h30: In the vicinity of the Mapetla Garage at the Orlando West-Meadowlands intersection; two Putco buses were set on fire. A crowd of between 5 000 and 6 000 was rioting in this area.

17h50: A Putco bus and a motor vehicle from Perkins Truck Hire were burnt in the vicinity of Uncle Tom's Hall.

A control room was set up during the night at the WRAB head offices in Albert Street, Johannesburg.

18h00: A classroom at the Naledi High School was set on fire.

A bottle store in Klipspruit was looted. Tear-gas and firearms were used to disperse 400 Blacks.

The Urban Bantu Council building in Jabulani was set on fire. The fire was put out, however, as was the fire at the Sebokeng Garage.

Two motorcar wrecks were placed on the Phefeni railway section in order to block it. These wrecks were removed by the Railway Police.

19h00: The police split into smaller groups, who were assigned specific tasks. Brig. Le Roux, accompanied by a number of armed men, went by motorcar from the Moroka Police Station to the Jabulani Police Station because communication between these stations was poor and there was no telephonic communication. Their motor vehicle was pelted by stones and one of the windows was shattered; the roads were blocked by burning wrecks. The Divisional Commissioner remained at a looted bottle store in Jabulani till 21:00 to take charge of police operations against the large-scale rioting in the area.

19h45: The Phomolong Bottle Store was looted by about 300 men. The police shot and wounded an inciter, who was stirring up the bystanders.

19h50: Four hundred rioters were milling around the Mapetla Garage in Orlando West. They threw petrol bombs at vehicles and petrol pumps. On arriving there, the police were attacked and they opened fire on the attackers. Two wounded or dead rioters were dragged away by their companions.

20h00: About 200 people went on the rampage, looting and setting fire to the Dube Bottle Store. There were cries of 'Kill the Whites'. The police are thought to have shot five persons. Fleeing rioters dragged away the wounded or dead.

Two men, one of whom a youth, were shot and wounded by the police at
the Mofolo Bottle Store.

21h00: A meeting of the Soweto Parents' Association was held in Dr A.M.
Mathlare's consulting-rooms. The meeting was under his chairmanship and
its purpose was to discuss the events of the day. Dr A. Mathlare,
Mrs W. Mandela, T. Motapanyane, a scholar, and Mr R.M. Matimba, a teacher
were among those present. Mrs Mandela proposed that a mass funeral
service be held on Sunday 20 June 1976, in the African Methodist Episcopal
Church for the police victims. The service was later prohibited in terms
of section 2(1) of the Riotous Assemblies Act, no. 17 of 1956.

22h45: The police found Barclays Bank and the library in Dube on fire;
the Board's offices had already been burnt down when the police arrived.
Members of the force were ordered to stand guard at the buildings.

23h00: A Black man, V. Nkwanazi, is alleged to have been shot in front
of the Carolina-Nvuzi Nursery School in White City. No further information could be obtained.

23h10: The bottle store in Phomolong (sometimes called the Phefeni
Bottle Store) was attacked by incendiary bombs. The police opened fire
on the attackers.

Chapter 6
17 and 18 June

SOLOMON MARIKELE, *Rhulane Senior Primary School*

Solomon:The following day I pick up stones. I joined the struggle. I did whatever we were supposed to do during [those] days, because we were burning everything, offices, you know, municipal offices mostly. Breaking schools, burning cars from the white man. As long as that thing belonged to a white man, we burn it.

Q: Does that mean on 16th June you went home and stayed home?

Solomon: On the 16th, I just came home and stay, but the following day, it's where things go the way they wanted us to do. To join them and to do whatever they were doing because we formed the slogan, we said: 'Injury to one is injury to all.'

So we were supposed to be there.

Q: How did you join the other comrades?

Solomon:The following day I saw the comrades passing next to my home. They are going on top there, they say: 'We are going there.' 'Niyabasaba na? Hayi asibasabi.' – 'Are you afraid of them? No, we are not afraid of them.'

We went to them. So they raise my spirit, I joined them, you go throw stones.

We burn everything, by the way. Whatever belonged to the apartheid government, we burn it.

Q: Tell me about your first action.

117

Solomon: On the 17th mostly it was youth who were doing these things, because adults were staying at the back, watching us what we were doing. We are doing in a right way ... the way they wanted us to do. I started throwing stones on the 17th till the day we stopped everything, the government started listening to us and said: 'Okay, no more Afrikaans by force, you learn the way you wanted to learn.'

But Afrikaans as a subject is still there.

Q: Did you personally participate in burning one of those government properties?

Solomon: I end up a ringleader when it comes to burning. I end up a ringleader, end up [with] the police coming and looking for me. I have run away. My mom took me to Qwaqwa and [I] stayed there for a long time. I came back after two years or three years.

Q: How did you lead the others?

Solomon: I was so aggressive. Once they see me, they know ... Now the corruption [has started], but it was not part of corruption. It was part of the struggle. So I don't want to see the comrades standing and watching. We have to challenge them.

Q: Did you have meetings before you went to stone cars or loot?

Solomon: There was no meeting. We meet there on the Potchefstroom [Road], then we started the action from there. There is no meeting, there is nothing. We throw stones when we see the white man's car is coming. Whatever we break, we burn.

Q: Did you ever see someone shot by the police?

Solomon: There were plenty during those days and they [were] youth mostly. There were plenty, I can't even name how many. On the day [there] are two, three injured. Someone is dead there, you know. You can't even understand why these white men [are] shooting the children. Why they can't listen to the children, what the children want.

Q: Were you aware of what you were fighting for?

Solomon: They have explained to us before they chased us from the classes. We won't do things in Afrikaans, because Afrikaans you'll use it in South Africa only. You wanted to go to the other country, they speak English there, you don't know English. So we wanted to do things in the international language so that we can co-operate with the whole world. So we take it from there.

118

Q: Did you participate in the burning of the bottle stores?

Solomon: The one which we have burnt and crash down, was that one from Senaoane because I was attending school at Sekano-Ntoane.

But it was during 1984 when we started these siyayinyova comrades. I was a member of the Congress of South African Students during those years and we started again because we see that this government is not listening to us in the full way, so we have to act. So we used to hijack Putco buses and crash that bottle store and take the liquor there. You know we drink and drink. We go to challenge the mayors, we burn their houses. You know, they wanted us to pay high rent and at the same time they do nothing for us.

Q: Did you attend any meetings in 1976?

Solomon: The people who used to call meetings during those years, [in] 1976, it was Azanian People's Organisation which were ruling the movement at the time. They were the people who told us that: 'We do like this, we do like this, we don't want a white man.'

The Black Consciousness Movement [said] things like that, 'Black is black,' you know, 'White is white'. Supreme is black, things like that.

SOLLY MPSHE, *Morris Isaacson High School*

Solly: I went to bed [on the 16th] knowing that the first thing to happen the next morning is to go to school. It was only in the morning that I realised that there is no way I can go to school. By the time I got up, people were running amok, carrying cases of beers. In under two minutes I knew that Merafe bottle store was broken into, it was catching fire slowly, and if I wanted some beer I had to fetch [it] from the bottle store.

I got there very early in the morning [of] the 17th and I managed to get some beers. I realised that since yesterday afternoon things were happening, but moved away to the centre. Merafe apparently was broken into the day before, in fact very late in the night. Some guys from wherever were joined by workers. [They'd] seen what was happening in the east as they went down to deep Soweto. That is when I started seeing slogans pasted on the wall: 'Viva ANC' and 'Amandla' and all those things. And the feeling was like, oh, the ANC is back in the country. Though later on I started questioning some of the slogans.

PRISCILLA MSESENYANE, *St Matthews School*

Q: What happened the next morning, 17 June?

Priscilla: We prepared ourselves to go to school and at nine in the morning it erupted again. We were told to go home by the principal. I hurried straight home and never met police on my way. We were using back streets, avoiding the area known as mochayineng, where most of the action was concentrated. I met a score of high school students singing and waving placards.

When one delivery van was being looted, I also grabbed something, viennas and polony which I took home. But we had to eat and finish them before my mother arrived. She would have been furious. She had strongly warned us not to go out of the house.

HENDRICK TSHABALALA, *Gazankulu Senior Primary School*

Hendrick: Before we reached the school, when we turned around that shop's corner, we saw a Hippo which was carrying police and soldiers entering in our school. We were frightened to such an extent that we stopped and relaxed at the shop. Then we saw some children coming out of school. When we asked them about what was happening they told us that they were told that there was no schooling on that day, therefore we went back home to stay.

We found that the bottle stores, shops, cars, bakery, buses – everything was messed up. It was mess. We wanted to make ourselves people by going to see for ourselves what was happening. We went further to meet other friends and started misleading each other [with rumours], we heard that they were coming from Rockville, Regina Mundi. Before we could reach Regina Mundi, by Esso Garage, we found that things were up and down. It was really busy, busy.

Q: Who told your schoolmates that there was no school?

Hendrick: They said that they were told by the soldiers. [The soldiers] did not try to give us any trouble.

Q: At which shop or store did you relax?

Hendrick: It was the one which is next to us here at Gazankulu, it is written 'Timhaka ti huma e Pitoli' (Troubles are coming from Pretoria). Ja, even in 1976 the same was written [on the shop].

As we heard the other children say that there was no schooling on that day we decided to go back home and change our clothes. [Then] it was business as usual. We took our soccer balls and went to the soccer ground. While we were at the soccer ground a certain man came and warned us not to play and also advised us to go back to our respective yards. Only to find that people like us were inquisitive, we never stayed or spent much time in the yards.

We decided that it was time for us to take a walk and see what was happening on the other side of Chiawelo. We went on and on and on playing with friends. Soldiers and police vehicles were roaming around, but [we] did not understand what was going on. Immediately when we reached the mountain [koppie] we met the elder boys. They said to us: 'Hey, you children, where are you going?'

We continued ignoring them.

'Hey, go back and don't walk in a mob, because when you walk in a mob like you are doing, they will suspect that you are also going to do something, you are going to get injured. Do like this when you go back … you must be separated.'

Because of the respect we had for the elders, from the mountain [koppie] back home we separated, each and every one of us was walking alone until we met at the very same corner which served as our point of departure. From there I entered the home, then it was: 'Gents, all right, sharp.'

From there I stayed at home until in the evening. I was so worried when I realised that my parents were not home and started to do the things which I usually did in the yard.

As I was worried [about] my parents, I decided to join other children who were going to Potchefstroom [Road], the place where everything was happening. I had a hope that I will be able to save my parents in case they are in trouble. Before we could reach the street that leads to the green church, it was like the whole of Soweto was in flames, cars and many things were burning. The police and soldiers were now shooting indiscriminately. People were stoning at the police and running at the same time, the same was happening to the police and the soldiers.

Something I found to be surprising was that the police attacked every child, whether he was causing havoc or not. The children were also attacking cars whether they belonged to the whites or not.

You mean to say black-owned vehicles were also attacked?

Hendrick: Ja, you know, so many innocent blacks, their properties were attacked. Throughout June 1976 I never stoned or looted anything, but I enjoyed waking up every morning to go where troubles were happening. I just enjoyed staying at the corner and watch things happen.

I felt bad, very bad, when I saw children shot [and] wounded, but I also felt bad when I saw the children stoning at innocent vehicles. It was ... as I said, a mixture of feelings.

STEVE LEBELO, *Madibane High School*

Steve: The next day was the 17th, we never went to school. It was a Thursday, and I never went to school on Friday. A lot of the activities that happened on the 17th and the 18th, especially in Soweto, were organised. A lot of the students were there, because they never actually went to school, but that's when police found themselves in clashes and skirmishes from time to time, with almost everyone in the township, including young adults, who were not working or who were not in school.

It was only on the 17th and the 18th, when police went out and systematically were killing people. I do know that suddenly there was the infamous green car. It was a 3800 Chev, it was a green car, and at the time they were used mostly by police. We suspected that they had a sniper in there, who picked up people at random and shot and killed them. I do know of a friend of mine who was killed on the 19th June, under the same circumstances. He had gone to the shop, and as he came back from the shop carrying a litre of milk, he was shot by a sniper and killed. He wasn't the only one, there were several people who got killed that way, under those circumstances.

But then the 17th, 18th, it's the end of the week then. At the weekend, we did actually play our sports. Except that police were a little uneasy about us being in groups, and a little later they passed a law which prohibited people from being together. Because we were playing soccer, they allowed that to happen, except that we started having games that were almost guarded by Hippos, soldiers, who were there to see that the matches began and ended, and there was no violence at all. So for some time we had that kind of a situation in Soweto.

With this kind of thing you have police confronted by students, and soldiers coming in, and initially you would have this kind of conflict situation, but over time, we came to accept the fact that these guys are here. So, I remember we played a number of games, and we just ignored them.

Q: When was the first time you heard about Hector Peterson?

Steve: It's funny, because I think it was a week, a day, maybe only three or four days later, when they said the youngest person shot, in the June 16th uprisings, was Hector Peterson. Maybe not even four days later, now that you ask that question. I have to think through it carefully, but I think it was much later.

Q: What part did he play?

Steve: I think it's a little unfair, you know, for people to say he was an innocent bystander, but at the same time I feel that it is overstating the fact, to want to make him a hero. There's no doubt that Belle Higher Primary School was one of the schools that would have been affected by the [language] ruling, and there is no doubt that Seth Mazibuko, who was the leader of the junior secondary schools and who led them on this march, had actually targeted those primary schools, because the ruling would have affected them much more than any other group of students at the time. So Belle School was there at the centre. I'm sure you've been to Hector Peterson's [memorial], it's [near] the school, just behind the square. It's also a central place, and like I said, this is a primary school where the ruling would have affected those kids for the rest of their high school lives. Therefore, it was pretty close to their hearts, but I don't actually think that they understood the dynamics of the march itself, and [it was] just like SASM (South African Student's Movement) drew them out of the school and said: 'We are going to march.'

It was just unfortunate that Hector Peterson was actually shot. In a sense, he wasn't an innocent bystander, he was drawn into it, yes, but I don't think he was conscious of what was happening at the time. I really don't even think that he anticipated what the police would do.

DINGANE LEBELE, *Madibane High School*

Q: Did you go school on the 17th?

Dingane: No. That is when the unrest began in Diepkloof. That is where I left school forever. We were no longer respecting our teachers. Mehlape, who was the principal, could not do anything to us. We were no longer listening to him. We were burning beer halls, post offices. We were throwing stones at police. Hippos were coming into Diepkloof.

Q: Do you remember going to meetings in 1976?

Dingane: It was at Madibane High School in 1976. But that was after we had burnt down beer halls and post offices. That is when I took to drinking. I started drinking liquor at that time. I still drink to this day. That was on the 17th.

BAFANA HLATSWAYO, *Nonto Junior Primary School*

Bafana: I started to see real trouble on the following day. So many things were burnt down. I stay just in front of a bar, it was burnt down. It was burnt on the 16th, but I myself saw it on the 17th. There was no schooling and people did not go to work, that is the day which I became aware that there was something that was happening.

Q: Did you participate?

Bafana: Ja, I used to like these things, to be in the forefront. I was very active at my age. I did not join any organisation but I was a person who was running like any other child in Soweto, and I wanted to find myself in front of everyone. I wanted to find myself also on the streets throwing stones or stopping cars and all those things. I always knew that there was a company car which was to be burnt at so-and-so place. I would be there burning it or there is something to be taken, it is a target. I was always in the forefront.

Q: Which things were targets?

Bafana: I think government properties. Everything that belonged to the government at that time was a target; even a white person was a target. I personally was not able to recognise a target, but I could see that there is a car which had been stopped. I did not want to know whether it is a target or not, but when I saw a car stopped I would throw myself on it very quick, very fast.

The places we mostly targeted are places like Esso Garage which divides Dhlamini, Chiawelo, Senaoane. We knew that cars which travelled to Protea or Lenz or Potchefstroom and cars which went to town drove along those roads, Old Potchefstroom Road. That is the place we mostly [ambushed cars] and again it is the street at which the police station is situated. Imagine how brave we were at that time. We did not mind, see, that the police station was nearby.

Q: Tell me about the other properties you burnt apart from cars.

Bafana: I remember when I found myself inside the clinic looking for some things that I can't tell you what I was going to use for in case I got them. You know, [whenever] I saw a doctor, it was like I was seeing a very big thing. So I always wished I had that instrument he uses to check the patients. So I made sure that I searched all the un-burnt rooms looking for those instruments, until I found myself at the Chinese shopping complex. At mochayineng there was everything – meat, butchery, timber yard, firewood. I would always find myself there.

Before we talk about mochayineng, let's talk about this incident that traumatised me for the rest of my life. During the march through Potchefstroom Road, I remember there was one old lady, she was older than me, by the name of sister Baby. I was always in front of that lady because she was the one who pushed me, pulled me back, in case I moved or walked far forward from her. Somewhere where we had to run away from the boers, she was shot down, she was shot down. I remember well, I was in front of her and she was behind me when she was shot. You know, it was my last day to see her.

Q: Why, do you think she was protecting you?

Bafana: Ja, that sister was sure of what she was doing. She knew her things, always when tear-gas was shot at us as she would take out wet cloths and give us as young ones. We learnt from her how to weaken tear-gas. She would always teach us how to weaken tear-gas with water. I think [of] the way she always guided me in the right way and I did not know her.

Q: How was she shot?

Bafana: It is hard to remember the story of that sister because really, you understand, everyone was running, she got shot. I don't know how, the boers were just shooting in either way. The only thing I saw is the place at which I fell. [It] was next to a house fence, so I managed to see that my sister had fallen on the street. The boers came to fetch her. You know she [was] immediately raised, her corpse immediately raised. I won't tell you what kind of gun was used to shoot her. She was brutally taken and thrown into the police van. I saw the whole incident with naked eyes.

You know the way I was frightened, but funny enough it never stopped me from doing what I was doing at that time. It actually made me to be more crazy, because from that incident I managed to reach mochayineng's place.

Q: How did you get to know her name was Baby?

Bafana: I remember her name called in front of me. Some were shouting: 'Baby, Baby, Baby.'

And everyone was screaming: 'It is Baby! It is Baby!'

I did not know at that time this sister was Baby. It really took me two or three days to know that she was sister so-and-so and she stays at so-and-so place. It was not that I knew her because she was a neighbour. I did not know her. I only heard her name called 'Baby!' and also when various families talked about Baby of so-and-so place.

Q: As a grown-up do you still feel the way you felt when you were a child?

Bafana: Ja, too much. Sometimes I tell myself that if I were a little [more] grown up then maybe I could have done something to protect her, or since she is no more existing, I should be doing something for her family to show them that we did not forget her. Her spirit is still in us, because I feel very pity and guilty when people show me her child. I am even afraid to relate to her child how his mother died.

Q: Tell me about the type of car she was put in.

Bafana: These cars were commonly known as 'Kwela Kwela' or 'Gumba Gumba'. It was just a big truck with a lot of mesh. Everyone who happened to be arrested was just thrown into this truck. Some were put in sack, but she was just thrown inside the car. I really don't know what happened thereafter.

Q: On what day was sister Baby shot?

Bafana: She died on the 17th of June 1976.

Q: Did you know what was happening during those days?

Bafana: No, I won't say that I knew what was happening but the thing I mostly knew at that time was that we were fighting against the boers, we were fighting against the government, that is the only thing I knew.

THOMAS NTULI, *Nghungunyane Junior Secondary School*

Q: Tell me about the 17th.

Thomas: There is a garage next to my place called Esso Garage. When I wake up in the morning, there was a mob, picking up our hands, saying, 'Power, Power, Power'. Stopping cars, breaking some car windows. There came the soldiers. There is one sister who stays in Dhlamini. She was killed there on the 17th. You know, my first time to hear a gunshot was on the 16th of June. The second sound of guns [was] during the 17th. So I became used [to the sound] and we were using a lid of a dustbin – a metal one. That's why they changed it into rubber, because it could block a bullet at the time. We were too militant. Unarmed, we used inferior weapons, but we managed to survive.

Q: Besides the Esso Garage incident, in which other burning or stoning incidents have you participated? Beer halls?

Thomas: It was my first time to start drinking, to start touching beer. I don't know that kind of a beer, the bottle was called Golden Dice and Cola punch. You know, my first time to sip it ... the change in my mind, that wonderful glow, that excitement, you get it the first time you drink.

Q: Which bottle store?

Thomas: It wasn't exactly a bottle store, it was a lounge, Chiawelo Lounge. It was a 'bara' [beer hall]. We use to call it a 'bara'. It sold 'Mai-Mai' [sorghum beer] and all those things.

[The police] came after, they found some people busy there, shooting, tear-gas, killing some others, arresting some others. Ah, some of my friends are dead ... some of my friends are dead.

GANDHI MALUNGANE, *Nghungunyane Junior Secondary School*

Gandhi: In the morning, that's when I started to understand what was happening, and I joined now, I participated fully now. I fully participated after that day. The parents, they gave us the go-ahead. My mother wouldn't say: 'Where are you going?'

She would just say: 'Be careful.'

The following day, the 17th, we started attacking. Believe me, I became a different Gandhi. I was dealing in this as well. I was taking charge from the 17th, no, the 18th, I took charge of the group, barricaded the roads.

Q: So you became a leader?

Gandhi: Yes. [At the age of] fourteen years. I remember when we went to burn the beer hall, I was there, as well as the bottle store, then there was a clinic. I participated in that as well.

Q: When did you hear about Hector Peterson for the first time?

Gandhi: On the 17th. I got it from the radio, and my father was always buying newspapers. I can't remember who told me, but one of the family who was staying said: 'There was a young boy shot yesterday.'

Q: How did you feel when you heard about that?

Gandhi: I felt very bad about it. I felt very, very bad about it, and very sad about it. The death of Hector Peterson, and the others, it made me to feel like fighting until I die, because I saw people dying next to me and in front of me. On the 17th, 18th, I saw people dying, but I couldn't give up, because we were prepared to die, like the song said: 'When we die, we go forward.'

TONY HANYANE, *Tiakeni Junior Primary School*

Tony: I had a friend of mine by the name of Solomon Marikele. We were doing the very same class during that day and during those years. He lost his tooth from tear-gas which was shot directly to his face by the soldiers. It was a tear-gas which automatically exploded in front of his eyes and he ended up colliding with me and collapsed. We had to lift him up and save him so that they cannot come and get him.

Q: Did you go to school on the 17th?

Tony: From the primary side everything was all right, because we knew nothing by then, but from the secondary side there was now starting to be divisions among the students. Some [were] saying, okay, Afrikaans is fine. Some saying, Afrikaans is not fine for us.

GEORGE BALOYI, *Nghungunyane Junior Secondary School*

Q: When did you know of Hector's death?

George: On the 17th and it was said he was shot on the 16th. We were told that there is a boy who was shot and he is called Hector Peterson. In fact he was not alone. Yes, he was not alone. There is another one, I just forgot his name.

Q: Was it at the same place?

George: At the same place. The only name that appears was that of Hector Peterson. The other one's name did not appear. Even the camera shot only Hector Peterson.

Q: How was the other child shot?

George: Well, he was also one of our groups, but he was on the side of Hector Peterson and Tsietsi, but it was the same time and the camera just happened to focus on Hector Peterson and the other one was unfortunate with the camera.

Q: How did you feel about Hector's death?

George: We were not frightened. It never stopped me from throwing stones.

MARTHA MATTHEWS, *Kelekitso Junior Secondary School*

Q: Tell me about the 17th.

Martha: The following day it was worse because these boers were now following people inside their yards. We could not go out. We could not go buy in shops. There was no person who [was] walking on the streets. It was bad, bad. I still remember children crying for bread. There was no chance of going to spaza shops because the boers' cars were patrolling, and they were driving very slow, very slow. I am telling [you], if you want to die just get outside the house. Even if you are not doing anything, they would shoot you, for as long as they meet you on the road. They used these green cars, some of them were called Hippos. They were green but not this bottle green. [It's] green like the post office or prisoners' uniforms. They were patrolling the children. As long as they realised your age, that you're fit to be a schoolgoer, you were in for it. They could even shoot a toddler as young as six years. That was on the 17th, 18th, 1976, it continued. It was now very bad. 17th, 18th was more than the 16th, because just meeting you on the street they shot you. They were no longer using rubber bullets.

Q: Which properties were looted in your presence?

Martha: In Meadowlands it was a bottle store, a post office and the rent office.

Q: Where were the police?

Martha: When they arrived it was already burning. It was already burning to such an extent that there was nothing they could do. There was no help they could offer.

Q: How did you feel about the whole thing?
Martha: Embarrassed.

THAILANE NGOBENI, *Nghungunyane Junior Secondary School*
Q: Tell me about the 17th.
Thailane: The following morning when we came back everything was burnt down. We even organised some of us to warn the parents not to go to work. I warned my mother by myself, in person. My mother's name is Regina Ndebe, the same night I told her not to go to work. She was working night shift, I said to her you cannot reach your workplace. My father had already gone to work, because he was doing day shift, but he came very late that day.

What was burnt here in Chiawelo on the 16th was Chiawelo bottle store, Chiawelo bar. On the 17th Senaoane bottle store and office were burnt.
Q: Were you there at Senaoane?
Thailane: On the 17th we went to Senaoane bottle store, and there is no one who can tell me shit, I am sorry to say that. There is no one who can tell me nonsense or what, what, [the one who burnt] Senaoane [bottle store] was the last one, the one who survived was called Matrix Banda. His father was selling newspapers at Chiawelo station. While the bottle store was burning the boers arrived, he hid himself in the ceiling [and] he survived. How? We don't know.

Matrix is still alive and he is working as a cable specialist, but I can't tell you where he is working. He is a good chap and he is shocked to see me alive in South Africa.
Q: So you were still in Soweto on the 17th?
Thailane: On the 17th I was still around, but after having realised that I was in danger, that Norman Sunduza and Mawila are searching for me, I fled to my brother at Zola. Zola is a big place …

From there I became a wanted boy. I went to Zola, I went to Jabulani. I was hiding in my hiding places. So I decided, somebody decided, that you must move because you are wanted. In Chiawelo more especially [since] you've organised how to produce a petrol bomb. So I went to Springs; from Springs, Swaziland; from Swaziland, Matola in Mozambique.

I stayed [in Matola] for five months. I went to Angola, I was trained.

130

They insisted [on this] during the time of Joe Modise. They told us: 'You are still young.' Even now you can see I am still young.

I said: 'I want to go and use the gun in order to relieve or release our people who are under apartheid. We are still young and therefore we will fight.'

We were promised that we will be tomorrow's leaders. We will govern the country as long as we defeat the system. Well, I went there. They even took me to Germany, Angola, Russia, Tanzania, Zambia ... I was there, everything.

Q: When did you hear of Hector's death?

Thailane: As far as I'm concerned, the time when Hector Peterson was shot, we did not know. All of us were stopped by the police with their helicopters, Hippos, Land Rovers ... on the roads. So we went to town, New Canada, so many places. So about Hector Peterson, I'm sorry, I just heard about it.

TULU MHLANGA, *Tiakeni Junior Primary School*

Tulu: The only march that I followed was the one during which we were turned away by the police in New Canada.

Q: When was that?

Tulu: I cannot remember well, but [it was] the very 1976. If I can remember we were going to Booysens. I think we were sending those memoranda. Remember I was at primary level; we were just following without any clear knowledge. I was no more knowing the direction to go back home, I was just taking cover following the brothers. I knew they were coming from Chiawelo somewhere not far away. We found a kombi which was waiting. We all got inside the kombi. But they only allowed me in after I told them that I was from Chiawelo.

Q: Which routes did you follow?

Tulu: I can't remember well. Although I was born here in Soweto, I was not yet very clear about Soweto. I only remember when we were in New Canada, we were on the mountains. I hop [across] that street, the one that leads to Orlando. So we went to the likes of Nancefield, Mzimhlope hostel, and it took us back to Meadowlands. So after jumping the very same street, we were now there on the mountain [koppie]. We found that the police were many, then tear-gas was all over us.

Q: Which route did you follow back home?

Tulu: In coming back, I was just following those brothers I knew were from Chiawelo. I finally saw them entering a kombi. I don't know whether the kombi was hired or not. So I just threw myself inside. It is possible that it was hired because the driver was aware [of] who was getting off where. So-and-so was getting off in so-and-so place. I don't know if the kombi was hired or hijacked, mostly people who were inside knew one another, including the driver, because he could not ask where were we going to, he just drove off. We came back via Orlando, Nancefield and we came to Kliptown. I alighted at Dhlamini.

After that June 16, at school, I can say that it was beginning to go down, respect on the teachers. [Students] also told themselves that you are now political.

Q: At New Canada how did the police confront you?

Tulu: When we were marching [in] that direction the police came in front of us and started to shoot tear-gas and rubber bullets. Some of the group members were falling down. I really can't tell whether some died or not.

Q: When did you know that there was a child who was shot by the police and happened to be Hector Peterson?

Tulu: I heard of him on the 17th. They were talking about him and he was appearing even in the pictures.

Q: How did you feel when you heard of Hector's death?

Tulu: It frightened me a lot because Hector Peterson was younger than me. So imagine seeing a young child shot. I was feeling bad. [But] the event made me strong and [I] got deep in the struggle ... only to find I did not have enough education. But I ended up loving the struggle.

SAM ZIKHALI, *Ibhongo Junior Secondary School*

Sam: The truth is I was only a spectator. I was moving with any group and being a spectator. I don't remember myself throwing a stone or looting. I don't take anything that does not belong to me.

Q: How was the situation?

Sam: I was moving around the groups, changing from this group to that group, to that mob to that mob, right up to Orlando.

The other day when the march was organised and I joined, then I was part of it and we found ourselves in a certain house because of the tear-gas. There was an old wardrobe outside. So we went into this wardrobe. I saw this soldier coming, carrying a gun, and he pointed the gun at us.

One friend of ours said: 'No, baas, is nie ek, my baas, is nie ek, my baas.' By the name of Walter, he said: 'Is nie ek, my baas.' (It's not me.)

And then [the soldier] asked them: 'As dit nie jy is nie, wie weet wie het my met die klip gegooi?' (If not you, who threw the stone?)

And we didn't understand what was he talking about at that time.

And [Walter] said: 'Dit is nie ek,' and fell on his knees, and said: 'Dit is nie ek, my baas, is nie ek.'

So the poor [soldier] said: 'No well ...'

He saw that these three guys are young and he wouldn't afford to shoot them.

So he said: 'Slaap.' (Sleep.)

So we pretended to sleep and he left us like that.

We came back late at night, say about nine, because now we were afraid of these boers. We came back, walking from Orlando all the way, hiding. If we see a car we have to dodge and hide ourselves right up to the 19th day.

DAN MOYANE, *Morris Isaacson High School*

Dan: The following day I went back to school to hear what's the next step.

Q: But your parents, did they wake up and go to work on the 17th?

Dan: Azikhwelwa (We do not go to work) didn't start that day, but there was a lot of ... official intrigues – 'you are not going', but there was a lot of confusion about what's going to happen. But we knew we were not going to go to class, it was very clear that there would be a meeting. Parents were not sure what's going to happen. Other parents who heard about it left their workplace earlier and I'm sure some of them went back to work and their bosses told them: 'You don't have a job any more.'

So I can't recall exactly on the 17th, if my parents went to work or not, but I remember going to school and there were meetings, people were talking: 'What's next ...' And Azikhwelwa came up, boycotts, school boycotts, things were now spoken about.

Exactly what I did on the 17th ... I went to school in my school uniform and there were a lot of police. We could see Hippos, things we've never seen before. So even at stations there was a lot of control, and I know that my mother was very uneasy at that time. My father did go to work, I remember now. Ja, my father is just like that. He went to work and we went to school.

There were talks, there were rumours that Tsietsi has been arrested, you know those kind of things you get at a meeting. He had not been arrested then. I think it was a week, that following week, the following ten days, that the SSRC was officialised as a Soweto Student's Representative Council with every school being represented on it. I took part in one of the meetings around the time towards the end of the year, with Tsietsi talking about the way forward before he left.

Q: But there was no school in between?

Dan: No, schooling was disrupted; it was on and off. You know what happened – we would be sitting in class, after that sometimes just have a meeting, just say: 'Hey, there's a meeting.' We all left and we go to the hall, and the teachers would go to the staffroom and wait. Some teachers were not happy, they would challenge us, and we would say: 'No, no, we must have a meeting.' It went on for quite some weeks. And we did write Form Four (Grade Eleven) exam at Morris in November.

Q: As in November 1976?

Dan: Ja. Mathabathe is an educationist, I think he got a deal from the leaders to say we should be writing. I wrote my Form Four (Grade Eleven) in '76, and I passed.

I think there were promises made, that the government will discuss the Afrikaans issue, but by then things were going too far, there were people organising for the year ahead. At school, Morris, I remember we wrote Form Four, because we passed to go to Form Five (Grade Twelve) in '77, and that was the year when things didn't really work out well. I even volunteered to help Form Four, because we had so much disappointment, and some of the teachers were not available. Things were really getting ... the wheels were coming off in that sense.

Form Four is easy to write, because it's an internal examination, we were dependent on internal factors, you know.

PHYDIAN MATSEPE, *Orlando High School*

Q: On the 17th what happened?

Phydian: We didn't go to school. We just attacked anything that belonged to the whites. That day our first target was a bakery van, the police came and dispersed us.

Q: What was your first experience with tear-gas?

Phydian: I didn't know what it was, I was just amazed at this smoke.

Q: How did you feel about black policemen who were part of the group that was shooting at you?

Phydian: There was this one policeman, Hlubi, he was very notorious and we wanted to bring him down. Others were okay, we used to discuss some of the issues with them. There was also this policeman, Lebelo, who lived in Zone One. He was very famous for catching criminals. He told us that they couldn't resign. They [were] told that if they resign they will be locked up.

Q: What happened on the 18th?

Phydian: The shops were closed, we had a very bad weekend. There were no deliveries and people were hungry. But we shared what we had with our neighbour.

SOLLY MPSHE, *Morris Isaacson High School*

Q: Tell me about the police at the Merafe bottle store.

Solly: There were no policemen. There was no sign. That was the 17th in the morning now. I think they were shocked also. Suddenly everything was burning in Soweto. And even fire brigades were not trying to do anything. I don't know in some other areas, but I know that when they recovered, already damage was done. By the time the South African policemen decided to act, Soweto was too big for them.

By the 17th, eight o'clock, people were still having [a] free-for-all. In those bottle stores or beer halls or what you can call them. I remember I went back there again, the same day. I think nine-ish in the morning, ten-ish. The people [who] were trying to break in at that time were brave because [the] fire was getting a bit serious. [At] about that time there was no sign of policemen. So, if they took control overall, it must have been very late on the 17th in the evening.

Q: Tell me about the night of the 17th and the whole of the 18th.

Solly: I think from the 17th, 18th, things were actually spreading to the other neighbouring townships. Like Katlehong ... when you read the newspaper, the whole thing is spreading to areas like Katlehong and Mohlakeng and Kagiso. As things were calming down in Soweto, there were eruptions of violence all over Gauteng townships. When you thought [that] now things have stabilised, you could hear that something is happening in Carltonville, Springs. From the 20th onwards in June until the end of June, violence was spreading and continuing. In Soweto, the system intensified their security and patrol.

We spent most of those days indoors. That is when we started really to talk about politics. That is when we started talking about the ANC, the PAC, Umkhonto we Sizwe. And getting really interested in black consciousness. In fact I would say [that] during those days, black consciousness was [more] popular than these outlawed organisations. We started talking about guys who were in the South African Student's Movement, people who are in the South African Student's Organisation, the Black People's Convention, you know. That is when we really started relating politics and our situation.

Q: When did you know that the person who died was Hector Peterson?

Solly: I learnt the next morning in the newspapers that a thirteen-year-old boy was shot dead. That was the 17th. I think his name was later reported to be Hector Peterson, but the name of the boy came to my knowledge a day or two later. I am not quite sure because it was not so important. I think on the 17th the name was not there. It was just the years of the boy. Ja, they reported him as 'a thirteen-year-old boy from a neighbouring lower primary school', if I remember the wording correctly. On the 18th they put the name to the years.

Q: How did you feel?

Solly: I felt a bit angry looking at the age of the boy. And knowing that boy could not even harm a fly. Why put a bullet ... but I got worse when I saw the picture. You know the famous picture, the popular picture, where this guy is holding this boy and there was a young girl running next to them, crying, her hands up. Like she didn't know what to do. Ja, that picture sort of brought everything back.

I think that picture had a force to say, even to the guy who pulled the trigger: 'Why did you do it?'

I think that is the picture that made me to be angry and hate the system.

Top: 1976: An out-of-focus photograph taken of a confrontation between several women and the police aptly reflects the chaos of the moment. Photo: Bongani Mnguni

Bottom: 1976: A huge crowd milling around in the courtyard of the Regina Mundi Church. Inside, the church could accommodate 2 000 seated people and about 5 000 people standing. The number plate indicates the car was registered in Germiston, so people clearly came from outside Soweto to show their solidarity. Photo: *City Press*

Top: During the weeks and months which followed 16 June 1976, young students in casual clothes roamed the streets of Soweto. Times were tense and too uncertain for them to return to school and they had nowhere else to go. Photo: *Rapport*

Bottom: 1976: This aerial photograph of a winter's afternoon in Soweto, in late June or July when darkness fell around six o'clock, shows a typical scene at the time: a group of people watching a heart-stopping scene being played out around a Volkswagen kombi. At the time kombis were not yet used for mass transportation. Photo: *Rapport*

THURSDAY, 17 JUNE 1976
West Rand: Soweto

00h15: The West Rand Administration Board (WRAB) regional offices, situated behind the Meadowlands Police Station, were set on fire. The Police fired warning shots and used tear-gas to disperse the crowd present.

03h00: The Railway Police found the Inhlazane Station building, which had been attacked by rioters, in a badly damaged state. The body of a Black man who had been shot dead was found in the ticket office. Attempts had been made to crack the safe. When the South African Police investigated, they were pelted with stones. In the vicinity of the station everything was chaotic and the streets were littered with broken bottles and burnt-out vehicle wrecks. The beer hall near the station was in ruins.

06h00: The Railway Police received a report that the beer hall near the Naledi Railway Station was being attacked. On their arrival, they found that a number of men, women and children were carrying off or drinking the liquor. Some looters fled, but others pelted the police with stones.
    A signal box two kilometres from the Naledi Railway Station was burnt down.

06h30: Approximately 12 shops in the Klipspruit area were ablaze.
    A Black man, A. Gincana, was stabbed by an unknown Black, who identified himself as 'Black Power', on the football field between Moroka and Jabavu.

07h00: The WRAB offices for Areas 2 and 3, Meadowlands, were set on fire.

07h30: A WRAB sanitary depot in Area 2, Meadowlands, was set on fire. The police arrested a number of persons.

07h50: Pupils were milling around in the street in front of the Selelekela Secondary School. Some of them stopped motorists and forced

139

them to give the Black Power salute. The police dispersed the crowd and fired a number of shots.

07h50 to 09h20: After a beer hall in the area had been destroyed, about 3 000 rioters attacked the Naledi Railway Station. A senior officer of the Railway Police tried in vain to talk to the rioters; he was driven off with stones on five occasions and was also wounded. A white motorcar carrying four Black men approached the scene at speed. The hooter was sounded, the occupants gave the Black Power salute, and bottles with unknown contents were distributed to bystanders. Warning shots by the police had no effect. Someone in the crowd fired at the police with a small calibre firearm. Three of the inciters were singled out and shot by the police. The group retreated but later regrouped. Shortly afterwards police reinforcements arrived. A non-commissioned officer of the Railway Police was injured in the attack.

Four bodies with gunshot wounds were found by the police in the veld near the Naledi Railway Station.

Two bodies were found in the veld at Zondi. Another body was found half an hour later in one of the WRAB buildings.

The police found a body with a gaping chest wound in a house in Orlando East. The man was allegedly stabbed the previous night at approximately 20h00 by an unknown Black man.

08h30: A large crowd of about 1 300 persons was milling around in Masepha Street, Orlando East. Youths in school uniform were among those present. The crowd attacked the police with stones and the police used firearms and tear-gas.

08h35: A private motor vehicle was burnt out in the vicinity of the Orlando West High School.

A television newsman and a colleague were attacked in the vicinity of Baragwanath Power-Station. Their motor vehicle, carrying photographic equipment, was set on fire, but they escaped with the help of a Black motorist.

09h00: At the Indigihze Bottle Store in Dobsonville, five White members of the police force were surrounded and threatened by about 500 rioters. After police reinforcements had arrived, the crowd swelled to approximately 1 500. There were many scholars and youths in the crowd. Stone-throwing increased. The police fired warning shots over the heads of the rioters, without effect. Three men and a woman constantly incited the crowd by, *inter alia*, gesticulating and giving the Black Power salute. The four inciters were wounded by the police. One died afterwards. The crowd dispersed, and the police then found two more wounded persons on the scene. The police were not responsible for their wounds. The other wounded were arrested and taken to hospital. The vegetable-market in Orlando West was looted by a group of youths, but they were driven off by the police.

The Bogari Bottle Store in Dobsonville was looted and set on fire. Three rioters were shot by the police and a number were arrested.

The WRAB offices in Klipspruit were set on fire.

During the morning Credo Mutwa, the well-known writer and witch-doctor, a resident of Soweto and employed by the WRAB as cultural affairs officer, made an appeal over Radio Bantu to the public to restore order.

09h10: The police shot dead two persons in a stone-throwing crowd at the WRAB office in Diepkloof.

09h20: The administrative offices near the Potchefstroom Road in Klipspruit were looted. The police shot three looters dead and wounded three.

09h30: A Black girl, H. Leroke, was shot dead in Area 4, Diepkloof, after she and other bystanders had seen a helicopter and fled. One of her companions cannot describe or determine the origin of the shot; she did not see any police in the area. It would appear from this witness's statement that bystanders were looting a bottle store.

09h45: The Zola and Moletsana Bottle Stores in Jabulani were set on fire and destroyed. Two persons were shot dead by the police in these incidents. One of the deceased was identified as Charles Phakathi.

09h55: About 600 rioters took part in rioting at the Diepkloof Hotel. A lorry was set on fire, and incendiary bombs were thrown at the hotel. Police fired on the members of the crowd to disperse them. Five bodies were found on the scene after the incident. The police stated that two of the deceased were not shot by them because they had not fired in the direction of the place where the bodies were found. The deceased may have

141

been dragged there or could even have gone there themselves before dying.
A Mrs O. Mithi was walking to the hospital with two of her children,
Lily and Martha. In the vicinity of the hotel, the police fired at a
group of rioters. Both her children were hit by bullets, with fatal consequences in the case of eight-year-old Lily.

10h00: Members of the Railway Police on protective duty at the Merafe
Railway Station were surrounded by 2 000 rioters and attacked with
stones. A lorry at the station was set on fire. Passengers in the trains
were struck by stones. A beer hall to the east of the station was
looted. Two cars arrived on the scene; the hooters were sounded and, as
had happened earlier in the morning at Naledi Station, the occupants gave
the Black Power salute and distributed bottles (the contents óf which
were unknown) to members of the crowd. The attack intensified. A policeman was wounded. A Black man, Elijah Montjane, was shot dead by the
Railway Police during the attack. Presumably a Black boy, D. Mahasha, was
shot in the same vicinity between 11h00 and 13h00. Two inciters were
wounded by the Railway Police. Tear-gas was used to disperse the crowd.
   The Moroka Bottle Store was looted by rioters. Police used firearms
and arrested 25 rioters.
   The Iketlo Post Office was burnt down.
   The WRAB library and office in Area 1, Meadowlands, were burnt down.
The rioters were dispersed with the aid of firearms.
   The Diepkloof Beer Hall was set on fire. One rioter was shot dead.
   The WRAB maintenance offices in Orlando East were burnt down. The
police used firearms to stop the rioting.
   Major-General Kotze and Brig. Le Roux went on an inspection flight
over Soweto. They could see that large crowds were milling around and
that arsonists and looters were active everywhere. The streets were barricaded with motor car wrecks, stones and other large objects. While
trying to stop the looting, the police were attacked by rioters.
   The pupils of the Madibane High School went on a march to Orlando.

10h45: The vegetable market in Orlando West was again looted by a group
of youths and was set on fire. The complex was surrounded by the police,
whereupon the youths ran into the building. Gas bottles exploding in the
complex intensified the fire. The police removed 14 youths from the building but are of the opinion that at least seven others were overcome by the
flames and burnt. No further information in this regard could be obtained.

10h50: A Black man was shot dead by the police near the WRAB offices in Diepkloof.

11h00: Rioters were milling around in Moroka. The police noticed a body in the area.

Shops in Dobsonville were burnt down. Two bodies with stab wounds were found in the area. The police gave the Commission no further information in this connection.

11h30: On the old Potchefstroom Road, motor vehicles were overturned and set on fire by rioters. Two rioters were shot dead by the police.

11h30 to 17h00: Shops in the Naledi area were being repeatedly looted. The police shot dead six persons in these incidents.

12h00: The police gave White scholars protection on their way from the municipal power-station to Johannesburg.

At a gathering in the street, Tsietsi Mashinini called upon children to stay away from school and parents to go on strike. He told bystanders to use force where this appeared necessary.

The area around Baragwanath Hospital was quiet.

The Kliptown Meat Supply Store was looted. The police shot dead two persons and arrested 10. Harrie's Fruiterer was attacked and the building burnt down. In police action in this incident, three men were killed and one was wounded.

Looters again appeared at the Chiawelo Bottle Store. The police shot dead one man.

13h10: A lorry transporting fuel was stolen but was later recovered.

13h55: The telephone exchange at the Iketlo Post Office was damaged by youths. The police investigated the matter but the culprits could not be found.

14h00: Scholars erected barricades in a street near Baragwanath Hospital. A Black taxi driver was assaulted by rioters in the area. Blacks taunted armed policemen at the pedestrian bridge in the same area, but the police did not react.

A White reporter from a local newspaper was pelted with stones in the Doornkop area.

14h15: The body of a Black man with gunshot wounds was found at Moletsane. There had been no police action in the area, but a lorry had burned out there.

15h00: A shopping center in Jabulani was looted. The culprits had already left when the police arrived.

The badly burnt bodies of two Black men were found in the Phefeni Bottle Store.

A Black man was shot dead by the police at the WRAB offices in Soweto.

15h20: Youths attacked a WRAB official in a motor vehicle with stones. He defended himself with a firearm and wounded a 16-year-old rioter.

15h40: The WRAB garage near the Roodepoort Road was broken into and a vehicle was stolen.

16h00: Maj. Viljoen made use of tear-gas to disperse the crowd to the east of the Meadowlands Police Station. On his way from this point to the Jabulani Police Station, he saw a Black man leap from a WRAB tractor he was driving, leaving it to crash into a house. It was later established that the tractor had been stolen from the WRAB's maintenance section.

16h30: The shopping complex at Klipspruit, which had been on fire early that morning, was again looted and set on fire.

A hostel in Jabulani was attacked and an office set on fire. Two persons were shot dead by the police in this incident.

16h45: A number of buildings were set on fire in Moroka during the afternoon. About 50 persons looted Best Motor Spares, while 300 looted the buildings opposite. The police shot dead one person, wounded two and arrested three. The looters pelted the police with stones. The fire brigade's attempts to put out the fire were hampered by rioters slashing the fire hoses.

16h45 to 24h00: A reporter visited the Orlando Police Station with two colleagues in the late afternoon. They alleged that they had heard screams from the charge office, seen arrested youths doing exercises under Black police supervision and also seen the same youths later load

144

bodies into a hearse. These allegations were denied by a non-commissioned police officer who was on duty in the charge office that night.

Motor cars were pelted with stones on the old Potchefstroom Road.

17h00: The market in Jabulani was looted. Three persons were arrested.

Three Black men were shot dead by the police near Barclays Bank and the WRAB offices in Dube. One of the deceased was identified as J.W. Zwane. Particulars are not known.

17h15: A large group of rioters were milling outside the police station in Meadowlands. An occupant of a yellow motor vehicle fired a number of shots at the police station. The crowd was dispersed with tear-gas.

18h00: The Diepkloof Hostel was again damaged and set on fire. Some of the vandals were arrested.

The clinic in Diepkloof was damaged by fire.

The WRAB offices in the some area were set on fire. The police shot dead one person, wounded two and arrested 11.

In Orlando East, a Putco bus was set on fire. One person was arrested.

18h12: The magistrate's offices in Meadowlands were set on fire. Three persons were shot by the police in this incident. At Johannesburg Inquest 1371/76 it was stated that eight Black men were shot dead in the area. Later the same magistrate's offices were attacked with stones. A police patrol arriving on the scene was also pelted with stones. One of the stone-throwers was seriously wounded.

19h00: Two Black men are presumed to have been shot by the police near the new Soweto Highway.

20h00: The WRAB offices in Area 9 and 10, Meadowlands, were set on fire.

A Black man was shot dead by the police in Meadowlands.

Three Black men were shot dead by the police during rioting in a shopping centre in Diepkloof.

21h00: The beer hall in Area 4, Diepkloof, was looted and set on fire. One of the looters was shot by the police.

22h15: An attempt was made to break into shops in Chiawelo.

22h30: The body of a Black man, presumably killed by members of the public, was found in Area 10, Meadowlands.

22h45: The body of a Black man was found near the Zola Bottle Store. The deceased was presumably shot during earlier police action.

23h30: The body of a Black youth was found in Soweto. The place where he died and cause of death are unknown.

23h50: Rioters stopped a motor vehicle on the Soweto Highway, pelted it with stones and set it on fire. Six persons were shot dead by the police in this incident.

24h00: A Black man, J. Mputha, was shot by the Inhlazane Railway Police while breaking into the ticket office.

The bottle store in Meadowlands was burnt down and looted during the course of the day. Ten persons were found guilty of stealing liquor from the store. They were sentenced to five years' imprisonment, three years of which were suspended.

Chapter 7
18 June 1976 to February 1977

DUMISANI NTSHANGASE

Imagine you have just stepped off a crowded train onto the platform of Phefeni station at midday in early June 1976. You wander down the street, soaking in the rhythms, sounds and sights of people preparing for the weekend.

Fridays were not ordinary days in Soweto. They were the last day of the working week, or if you wish, the first day of the festive weekend. This is when alcohol, in gallons, was bought and consumed, and when stokvels – township savings schemes where money changes hands – took place. Stokvels were the most awaited events in any township in Soweto. The more popular you were, the more people were going to come and buy your stock. The more they bought your stock, the more money you made. The more money you made, the better were your possibilities of servicing your debt.

Weekends in Soweto started at Friday lunch-time at work or school. Most people were paid weekly so most of the people who were lucky enough to be employed had been paid by lunch-time. The first thing you did after getting your wages was to pay the mashonisa – a money lender who lent money at 30 per cent interest. After paying the mashonisa, you asked for more money from him. Once that four-minute exchange was over, you relieved your financial woes with a couple of quick gulps of beer or a painful swallowing of brandy or gin, just to get you back to work.

If you were a student, by lunch-time on Friday, there should have been no school. Why should there be school when everybody was waiting to spend the next two days without school? Teachers started preparing their throats for a few sessions of collegiality at the nearest shebeen and students anticipated attending a movie at Sans Souci in Kliptown or at the various small cinema houses like Eyethu in Dube. If you were clever enough you might have bribed your way to watching blue movies in the 'Evening Sessions' or sneaked your way in to a shebeen or stokvel.

Stokvels and the shebeen vibes started at about 7 p.m. By that time, everybody should have been back from work and away from nagging wives and undisciplined children. This was a man's world. Men drank in shebeens and stokvels but women were let in by invitation only. Sometimes a lucky wife got to go along. Otherwise, it was girlfriends or single women looking for guys who could buy them liquor for the evening in exchange for a few hours of sex.

Fridays were also significant in Soweto because they preceded Saturdays and Sundays. Saturdays were important because they were the days when young men woke up in the morning after a long drinking Friday. *Stlamatlama*, or hangover for the uninitiated, was a good reason to continue Friday's drinking spree. This started early, sometimes around 7:30, and ended around mid-morning, when everybody prepared for the rest of the day, either by starting a late morning snooze or continuing with the early morning binge until the body was unable to take it anymore. Sometimes, it took a fight to stop the binge. Someone would be hit with a bottle of beer or nip, a 340 millilitre bottle of brandy or vodka, or stabbed. Either he went home to be nursed by his loved ones or he was taken to hospital or the mortuary, if he was unlucky or weak.

Saturdays and Sundays were important for other reasons too. Apart from the drudgery of attending church on Sundays just to please your parents or show God that you could spare a few minutes for Him, Saturdays and Sundays were football days. Everyone wanted to watch players like Jomo Sono and Ace Ntsoelengoe. Who can forget the ululating sounds of female fans and the smell of marijuana smoked with bottle tops? If there was no game involving professional teams like Orlando Pirates, Kaizer Chiefs, Moroka Swallows or Pimville United Brothers at Orlando Stadium or Jabavu Stadium, there definitely would be amateur soccer. This involved local or visiting teams on the local dusty football pitches with invisible ground lines and no safety protection for the players or for the teams playing. Football – soccer, to be precise – was big in Soweto, and Saturdays and Sundays were the only days when good soccer was on display from both amateur and professional teams.

Sundays were important days for the ladies too. They were the only days when a woman got an opportunity to display her best dress and strut her stuff in the streets. Perhaps a few men would appreciate her or jealous women would talk maliciously about her out of sheer envy. Women gracefully adorned the streets in their checked skirts, maxi dresses and transparent floral blouses walking on 'three-steps', a type of ladies' shoes. Who would not want to be seen in a beret? It had to be black or blue, though.

Mothers and fathers spent most of their middle Saturday mornings and late Sunday afternoons attending self-help schemes and burial scheme 'society' meetings. Soweto was a big place and funerals were bound to be many. Weekends were also burial times. The mornings were spent assisting in carrying out funerals as well as lending a helping hand to the grief-stricken family.

Television had just arrived in South Africa. It was barely a year old. Apart from the curiosity about this new medium, people wondered how they could afford the necessary equipment. It was not uncommon to hear people saying: 'Now you will see all the people on radio instead of listening only to their voices.' The mystery of the voice and the face on radio was to be revealed.

But radio was still the most common medium of communication. Music and radio plays constituted the most popular form of entertainment. The young, as yet uncorrupted, and the old, waiting for their exit from here, joined together in the absence of those smelling of liquor and wandered through the incredible theatre of the mind.

However, if you stepped onto the station platform on the weekend of 18 June 1976, you would have found that things were different. You might have felt that it was a normal, sunny, winter weekend with a light breeze. But since Wednesday 16th, things had not been normal. Since Wednesday there had not been any order. Children had been killed by the police. The streets were filled with litter five times the volume of litter visible on New Year's Day. There were skeletons of buildings, near the burnt-out remains of what appeared to be a car. Many people were reported missing or held by the police. This was not simply another weekend.

For a start, there were no stokvels in Soweto that weekend. No stokvels at all. Not because they were banned or people boycotted them, but simply because it did not make sense to organise a stokvel when the police might be there to disrupt it. The government had declared that a gathering of more than five people was a 'crowd' and illegal. Six ordinary guys couldn't even get together for a drink.

In the immediate future Saturday was not going to be the same. There was no soccer. There was no soccer at all because only four people could play. So where did that leave the other 18 team members, 12 substitutes, one referee and the spectators? Anyway, how could there have been soccer games in such an abnormal weekend?

The weekend of June 18 will be remembered as the weekend that never was. While people drank liquor, as usual, the mood was far from festive. Dominating conversation among students was the question of what steps they were going to take. Conversation in families was about what they could do to ensure the safety of their children, how they could stop their children from causing more trouble and getting themselves shot or arrested, and more importantly, how they could ensure that they went to school and got an education. In the drinking groups, whether in shebeens or in small groups, the talk was the same: what was going on and where was it leading?

Interpreting what had happened the previous day meant trying to understand the context of what was happening. Understanding the context of what was happening resulted in an unprecedented increase in political militancy. Thomas Ntuli's brother was arrested that weekend.

Thomas: It was the 19th when he got arrested. [The police] arrested one boy who was called Haveline Manzini, in my very same street. So, he was beaten, that boy, by the police and he confessed: 'We've got our leaders at Nghungunyane, one of them is Morgan Ntuli.'

That is when my brother was arrested. They tortured him and all of that. Some of them were even killed at that time. Firstly, they took him to Kliptown, from there they took him to Protea where he was tortured.

From there they came to our place. They beat my mother, my sister and they searched the whole house. They needed some documents and all that. No documents were found. There was no exhibit of anything.

The dead are usually buried; there was no exception with the victims of June 1976. But the dead are usually buried within seven days of their death. The burial of the first victims of the events of June took place only on the weekend of 3 July, two weeks after the events.

For the families, burying their loved ones in peace was an important part of saying a final farewell. Families, friends and neighbours were informed and the process of burial was usually well planned. However, the victims of June 16 and the days thereafter, would not be buried like the other dead. Their bodies did not belong to their families. They were contested between the State, the families and the community.

Community members wanted to inscribe the bodies with messages for 'the struggle'. The State, however, demanded that the burials should not be political. While regular meetings provided for rational discussions and plans, funerals played on the emotions. This, the State understood. It gave specific instructions on how the dead should be buried.

The burials of Hector Peterson and the other victims were no exception. From 1976 onwards, funerals of victims of the police and soldiers became places for political mobilisation and emotional release. They ceased to be simple occasions in releasing the loved one to the ancestors. The bodies of the dead would no longer be inscribed with family memories, but would be a possession of the community and the struggle.

The months after June were filled with quite active political conscientisation, including reading books, attending meetings, holding sporadic informal political discussions and trying to figure out what to do the next day. One of the most important activities in 1976 was community theatre. On 30 June, many people gathered to watch the play *How Long* by Gibson Kente at the Donaldson Orlando Community Hall. But the play was prohibited by the Chief Magistrate of Johannesburg and could not be performed in terms of the Riotous Assemblies Act.

In Soweto, it was proving almost impossible to get back to a normal life. All schools had been officially closed. Family members started talking about what they should do to ensure that each member, primarily the young ones, got education. A number of families began to look out-side Soweto for relatives in the rural areas with whom their children could stay and where they would be able to attend school. This was the beginning of a great exodus from Soweto to boarding schools and schools in the homelands.

There were attempts to reopen schools in September, but without success. Schools were half-empty and this was not surprising. Such a long lay-off from schools requires a readjustment to a school mood. Even those who came back had their minds elsewhere. Rioting continued and intermittent chaos broke out in the townships. So students did not expect that schooling would return to normal for at least the remainder of the year. People continued to go missing, or were shot by the police. There was sporadic looting. In October, Mr TW Kambule, principal of Orlando High School, was quoted in *The Star* as saying: 'I wouldn't say the situation is back to normal here. Deep down there is anxiety, and it's difficult for students to study under such conditions. Some students, I am afraid, have just decided to quit school.'

Quit school? What does that mean? Looking for a job, looking for school outside Soweto or simply staying home and joining the hordes of the unemployed? Yes, any of these, but the option of going back to the classroom was the most difficult. Rioting continued. Now students went into exile in ever-increasing numbers. Thomas Ntuli recalls some of his friends who left for exile:

Thomas: We had one person called ... I forget his name. He used to take people to exile in coffins in order to cross the border, as if he was carry-ing dead bodies.

In November, *The World* reported that groups of students from Soweto had fled to Swaziland and Botswana, where they were seeking asylum. What was clear is that there was increased harassment by the state. If you decided to stay home, the police would forever be after you. You might be killed, indefinitely detained or simply disappear without trace. It was safer to go into exile and join the African National Congress, Pan-Africanist Congress, Black Consciousness Movement of Azania or any of those structures than to stay at home.

November was usually a month when parents planned the family December activities and expenditure. For sure, all children in the family must wear smart new clothes both on Christmas and New Year's Day. In addition, other family members, friends and neighbours should at least join you for a party on one of the December days, and there would be a lot of liquor and fun. Working people usually got their back pay and bonuses in November. Back pay and bonuses meant an extension of income and increase in expenditure. Pay all your debts, including mashonisa, put some money aside for the following year's new school uniforms and buy enough groceries to last until the next payday, the end of January.

During this time there were many attacks on various shops and bottle stores. There were also many attacks on schools and government and municipality properties. Anger had reached unprecedented levels in Soweto. However, events of ordinary days are important to individuals. Drinking, smoking, sex, early pregnancy, disillusionment with the future, hopelessness and chaos characterised life in Soweto. Almost everyone was 'political' at this stage. Solomon Marikele attended the first commemoration of 16 June in 1977 at Regina Mundi.

Solomon: My first meeting was at Regina Mundi, the following year in 1977. So I used to attend most of them. I used to be there. You find the police standing there, tear-gas, guns and all those things. Then, when the meeting is over, we asked ourselves: 'Niyabasaba na?' (Are you afraid of them [police]?) 'Hayi, asibasabi siyabafuna.' (No, we are not afraid of them, we want them.) We throw stones at them. We know they've got guns. We know they are going to shoot us. We know somebody is going to die, and we say: you die but your blood is watering the trees of freedom. So, it was our part of life.

How could children grow here? For Bafana Hlatswayo, June 1976 was the turning point in his life.

Bafana: Educationally it affected me because it reversed everything … It was like holding time for three years. Three years is not child's play. It's like being sent to jail for three years. I was affected spiritually, physically and practically.

Top: 1976: Bystanders in an unidentified street in Soweto watch smoke billowing from rubbish or possibly rubber tyres which had been set alight. The Cillie Commission Report into 'the Riots at Soweto and Elsewhere' states that when a certain Brig. Le Roux undertook an inspection flight by helicopter over Soweto at 14:00 on 16 June, the area 'seemed to be in chaos. People were gathering in several places. Vehicles as well as buildings were on fire, and parts of the area were under a pall of smoke.' Photo: Bongani Mnguni

Bottom: 1976: A police officer closely observes Bongani Mnguni photographing him and a plain-clothes colleague escorting a man towards a police Land Rover.

Top: 1976: A panic-stricken young woman fleeing clouds of smoke and tear-gas around the Regina Mundi Church. Fences often made it impossible for people to escape tear-gas attacks. For many it was the first time ever that they came into contact with this form of unrest control. Photo: Bongani Mnguni

Bottom: 1976: Young people choking from tear-gas try to escape by fleeing into the Regina Mundi Church, or through the church gate into the service road in front of the church which runs parallel to Old Potchefstroom Road. Photo: Bongani Mnguni

CILLIE COMMISSION
VOLUME II, pages 29–30; 46–47; 49; 293; 305 and 337

FRIDAY, 18 JUNE 1976
West Rand: Soweto

03h30: A petrol bomb was thrown at the Orlando Bottle Store.

06h30: The bodies of two Black men with gunshot wounds were found in Orlando East near a lorry which had veered off the road. It is not known who was responsible for their deaths.

07h15: A Black woman, Mothabeni Mabaso, was presumably shot dead by the police at the Chiawelo Bottle Store.

07h45: A shop in Kliptown was looted by rioters.

09h00: Mr J.C. de Villiers, West Rand Administration Board (WRAB) Chief Director, travelled through the streets of Soweto in a motor vehicle under police escort. He made use of an interpreter and a loudhailer, and asked the public to keep their children at home, because, according to him, conditions had degenerated into wholesale thuggery.

09h30: The body of a Black woman was found near the library in Meadowlands.

11h00: A Black man, H. Moleko, was presumably shot dead by the police at the Diepkloof Beer Hall.

11h10: A hall in Area No. 1, Diepkloof, was damaged. A rioter was wounded by the police and then arrested.

11h40: During rioting at the Soweto Wholesalers, police made use of firearms. Later, six bodies were found.

12h00: Two Black persons, R. Mayilange and J. Ndhlovu, were presumably shot dead by the police in Klipspruit. Mayilange was presumably shot at a Chinese store and Ndhlovu at another store. The records of Johannesburg Inquest 1371/76 stated, however, that their bodies had been found on the ceiling of the Klipspruit Meat Supply.

13h15: The market in Jabulani was again looted and set on fire. The police shot dead one of the rioters. At about 14h00, the body of a Black man, Bennet Mabuya, was found on the scene.

13h30: Three Black men were shot dead by the police in a bottle store in Dobsonville.

14h00: Following an invitation by the WRAB's Chief Director to Soweto leaders earlier that morning, a group of persons met at the WRAB administrative offices in New Canada to discuss the rehabilitation and reconstruction of Soweto. They included members of the Urban Bantu Council, White and Black churchmen, and other local leaders. The meeting was stormy at times, and the Blacks present asked to speak to the Minister of Bantu Education themselves.

14h45: Four Black men looted premises in Dube. The police arrested them. Two of the looters were wounded.

15h45: An attempt was made to set fire to the Zondi Store. Two of the arsonists were arrested and one was shot. Subsequently, the police also shot a rioter.

19h00: A police patrol shot dead one person when they came upon rioters looting a shopping centre. It is not clear from the evidence where this centre is situated in Soweto.

22h45: The police arrested nine persons at a store in Kliptown which had been burnt down.

SATURDAY, 19 JUNE 1976
West Rand: Soweto.

02h00: Calm had settled over the residential area. No rioting occurred during the day.

16h00: In Zola, the police found the bodies of four Blacks who had died from gunshot wounds. In three cases, the wounds had resulted from police action, probably during the previous day, because the police did not use firearms in that Saturday's rioting.

The body of a Black woman was found near the library in Meadowlands –
she was naked from the waist down, and there were indications that she
had been raped.

23h50: At about midnight, a Black man, who had smashed the windows of a
store and a house in Dobsonville, was shot by the police.

The bodies of five persons, who had presumably been killed by the police,
were left at various police stations and hospitals. It could not be
ascertained which one of them was killed in Dobsonville. One person was
shot dead by an unknown private individual. Seven persons died from
unnatural causes – their deaths are unconnected with the riots and were
not caused by the police.

SUNDAY, 20 JUNE 1976
West Rand: Soweto

Black motorists arriving at the police road-block in Booysens often gave
the Black Power salute to bystanders.
Two persons were killed by the police. No evidence regarding the circumstances surrounding their deaths is available.
A White woman, L.A. Scamotla, was injured on the Golden Highway by an
unknown stone-thrower. She died of her injuries on 30 June 1976 in the
General Hospital, Johannesburg.

What follows are random entries from the Cillie Commission Report which
ran to more than 200 pages

SATURDAY, 23 OCTOBER 1976
West Rand: Soweto.

12h00: About 1 000 persons assembled at the funeral of a schoolgirl, A.
Mkwanazi, who had died from natural causes. The principal of the school
attended by the deceased asked scholars from the school to attend the
funeral, to which they were transported in lorries. Inflammatory
pamphlets were distributed during the proceedings. After a senior police
officer had informed the crowd that the funeral could be attended by
relatives only, a part of the crowd became unruly and pelted the police
with stones. The police shot dead an unknown person, wounded another and

158

arrested 115 persons for attending an unlawful gathering.

In the case S v Meya and 28 others, which was a sequel to the above events, which had taken place in Mapetla, the charges against five of the accused were withdrawn; the remaining 24 were found guilty, two of them being sentenced to R50 or 50 days and 22 youths being sentenced to strokes.

14h00 to 23h15: Three incidents of stone-throwing at private and police vehicles were reported in Moroka, Naledi and Zondi.

MONDAY, 1 NOVEMBER 1976
West Rand: Soweto.

07h10: A Putco bus was attacked by a number of Black men. The bus was damaged, and the driver was seriously wounded with a knife.

10h00: A report was received by the police that a number of Black youths were pelting the railway station building at Limendlela with stones. When the police arrive, the youths had already left. Sixty-four window-panes had been smashed. The youths had gained entrance to the building and stolen R118 in cash.

13h00: A passenger train was derailed between Dube and Ikwezi Stations when a group of 12 or more persons placed rails on the railway line. The obstacle was noticed in time, and a serious accident was avoided. The accused in the case S v Khumbala, was charged in connection with this incident, convicted of sabotage and sentenced to five years' imprisonment.

18h00: A group of Black men stoned homeward-bound workers at the Merafe Railway Station. The police used shotguns to put an end to the disturbance.

18h05: Fires were started in coaches at the Phomelong and Mzimhlope Railway Stations.

19h00: Youths in Naledi tried to set fire to a Putco bus. The bus driver was robbed of tickets valued at R30.

19h30: Workers were stopped and assaulted by about 60 youths at Zola. Shotgun rounds were fired by the police.

TUESDAY, 18 JANUARY 1977
West Rand: Soweto

20h45: A fire in a classroom at the Thathezahlo School in Dobsonville
destroyed books, desks, shelves and other furniture.
At about the same time, two collections of books at the Maponyane
Secondary School in Meadowlands were destroyed by a fire.

WEDNESDAY, 19 JANUARY 1977 TO SUNDAY, 23 JANUARY 1977

No incidents were reported.

TUESDAY, 25 JANUARY 1977
West Rand: Soweto

13h15: About 45 youths smashed the windows of the Ikwezi Beer Hall and
set fire to a part of the building.

WEDNESDAY, 26 JANUARY 1977
West Rand: Soweto

Window-panes at the Helekanie Primary School in Chiawelo were smashed
during the night by youths.

THURSDAY, 27 JANUARY 1977 AND FRIDAY, 28 JANUARY 1977

No incidents were reported.

SATURDAY, 29 JANUARY 1977
West Rand: Soweto

03h00: Furniture and books in the Zisunelene High School in Orlando East
were set on fire with an incendiary bomb.

SUNDAY, 30 JANUARY 1977 AND MONDAY 31 JANUARY 1977
No incidents were reported.

160

Chapter 8
The aftermath

The long-term impact of the events of June 1976 on individuals actively involved and those drawn in by the sheer force they unleashed has yet to be explored. Most seem to be convinced that they emerged politically enlightened and have therefore benefited from the experience. They paid an immense educational price, however, for political enlightenment.

Solly Mpshe recalls how, as senior students, they repeatedly tried to return to school and complete their education. They never wrote their final examinations.

Solly: We didn't write [exams] ... there was no way. We tried to go back to school, to normalise things. In September we tried to march again. [By] that time there were structures which were formal, like the Soweto Representative Council (SRC). Tsietsi was still in the country and tried to march to Johannesburg, to release all those students who were detained since June 17. And there was a march to town ... and more students would be nabbed and basically we became more of politicians than school kids after June 16.

Ja, there was lots of disruption. We were spending more time outside the classroom. If we were in school it would be in meetings trying to understand what is happening. We had elected representatives to sit in the SRC. In our case that was a certain guy called Kenneth Mogame. He ended up being detained with the Soweto Eleven – that's what they called them. And I think in that period we saw three leaders over a short period of time. It was Tsietsi, he left, and then Kgotso took over. He was under pressure also and he had to skip the country, and there was Dan. Dan is now an activist with the ANC. I forget his surname.

We did it simply because the culture of learning was no more in place, between June 16 and October. Then the examinations were postponed to early '77. I recall that we wrote, I think January or February, by March we had to move to high school. There was no break in between. I remember we went to enrol before even knowing our results, just to secure a place. And when the results came out we were actually in Standard Nine (Grade Eleven) and there were other guys who had to go back to Standard Eight (Grade Ten).

Martha Matthews did not write her final examinations either. She remembers the way in which schooling was disrupted by the continuous police presence.

Martha: We did go to school. When the schools were officially reopened, we went to school, but the situation was no more good because there were always these attacks from the police. I blame the government, because if they did not threaten us, if they did not kill, if they did not make us paraplegics, we would have gone back to school. If [the] boers had handled it in another way we would not have died like we died, because even the soldiers were commanded, they were told what to do. That is why they had to shoot. That is why at a later stage soldiers from somewhere, the outsiders, were brought in so that they can shoot.

In spite of the way in which the political situation adversely affected her education at the time, she comments on her lack of knowledge in comparison to that of her elders.

Martha: I had no knowledge. I had no knowledge at all, because I did not understand this of Mandela, like my mother and father, they have been telling us the story of Mandela and Winnie Mandela, but of course I did not understand anything.

Muzikayise Ntuli did not attend school after June 1976. He never wrote his final examinations.

162

Muzikayise: We stayed 1976, '77, without attending school. The whole two years – in 1978 Standard Six (Grade Eight) was scrapped. When Standard Six was scrapped I went to Senaoane Secondary School.

Yet his political education had begun.

Muzikayise: Honestly speaking I got that after June 16th, but during 1976, because we used to have some meetings. There is no function[ing] of education at that time. We had to confront the system, because now we [were] at war [with] the minority South African whites [who were] killing us. There is no other way round [but] to continue fighting, to fight. I could see that there is a different Soweto and Johannesburg. In Johannesburg there are big buildings, in Soweto [I see] dusty streets, four-room houses, there was a difference.

Tulu Mhlanga succinctly describes the effect June 1976 had on him.

Tulu: June 16 had affected me too much. Yes, it affected me because it is where I started to realise that we must follow this road ... I must fight, we [must] fight the system.

I think I have gained from June 16, because through this June 16 I started to know that there are people like Mandela, they even come out of prison to become our presidents.

He believes that 16 June was an organised event, contrary to the popular perception that it was a spontaneous uprising.

Tulu: It was organised, because I saw what the leaders like Tsietsi [were doing]. During that march, each and every school they arrived at, students just followed. It means maybe there were meetings of the leaders.

Mhlanga's view of the woman teacher conducting a lesson in his class when school was disrupted on 16 June 1976 reflects much discourse about teachers and their role in the uprising. Apart from a distinct few who were considered 'politically informed', most teachers were seen as part of the system that students were beginning to abhor.

Tulu: The mistress who was teaching us that day, who criticised our fellow students who were carrying the placards, it was clear she was not politicised. Yet most of us understood a little about what was happening and that these people were rectifying something. I did not lose anything.

He alludes to the way in which funerals and attendance at funerals became politicised.

Tulu: From the 16th of June 1976, when they heard that there was a funeral, we used to attend those funerals, as well as the night vigils. When they said there was a meeting in so-and-so place, like Regina Mundi, we used to go and meet people like Bishop Tutu [then the Anglican Dean of Johannesburg] and the likes of Doctor Motlana [a prominent community leader].

The leaders were talking about the struggle. They politicised us about what was happening. When Tutu put it, he said one hand of a boer is holding a gun and the other is holding a bible. So when he hides a gun he takes out the one which is holding a bible so that we can read a bible.

Funerals became a major rallying point in the townships.

Tulu: We just sympathised, simply because we heard that he has been killed, maybe a schoolchild or so. We attended along those ways. I attended so many funerals. [When] I heard people saying: 'Let's go to the funeral,' I followed. [Who] the deceased was did not count. I attended too much. I attended even in Rockville, White City, I attended.

With the benefit of hindsight, was it right to get involved in the events of 16 June 1976?

Tulu: Yes, because now I am right. I am not working, but I've got something to make a living, and this was not possible during the boers' regime. I am looking, ready to be employed, when I happen to be employed. But now, meanwhile, I am not employed, I am able to feed myself enough.

There is a hint of tacit acceptance of his marginal economic and material circumstances. Tulu Mhlanga is convinced that he would have been worse off if apartheid had survived into the 21st century.

Other individuals affected by the Soweto uprising refer to sacrifices that they made. There is almost always a hint of a dream shattered by the events of 16 June 1976. This is what Vusi Zwane said:

Vusi: We were doing Standard Five (Grade Seven), on the 18th we had to go back to class. We went back, but it was not so normal because everybody, especially the senior students, they were no more learning. They were always drunk by the beers they have stolen in the bottle stores. So we were affected and as a result there was no more serious learning at the schools. But in December we did write the test. I passed and I got a 'C' symbol.

In 1977 they started something like Black Power. That is where the anti-white reaction started. People were no more allowed to buy from white-owned shops in town. There was no schooling for the rest of the year. Until December we stayed home. That is where we lost a lot of time. That is why they are calling us the lost generation. Even now I am still crying for that wasted year. If I went to school in 1977, I would be somewhere.

Dan Moyane had a dream which, he suggests, was compromised by the events of 16 June 1976.

Dan: I wanted to be a medical doctor, and perhaps a gynaecologist or a paediatrician, just to be with children. But, well, I did not. Because things fell apart. In 1978 it was clear in my mind that I had to do something while things were not clear. Because I wanted to finish some form of matric. So, if I have any regret, it is that I did not do a South African matric.

Taking a matriculation examination and obtaining a decent qualification was uppermost in the minds of many actively involved or caught up in the events of 1976. However, some considered sitting for a matriculation examination while their peers had been detained or killed as an act of betrayal. Phydian Matsepe asserts that he felt strongly about this issue when the government offered an opportunity to administer examinations in March 1977.

Phydian: In 1977 when examinations were written, these were 1976 examinations. This was early in 1977. I never wrote. I belonged to the group that [believed] it would be selling out to write examinations when other students are not there. Others did ... In August 1977 the government took over the running of schools from the communities. They said parents were unable to discipline children and schools became state schools. We never wrote examinations in that year.

Getting a matriculation qualification between 1976 and the end of 1978 became elusive for many. Like Dan Moyane, Phydian Matsepe yearned for a matriculation qualification. His quest for a matriculation qualification sent him to Herschel in rural Transkei in 1978, where the results were equally dismal.

Phydian: In 1978 many high schools were closed. The only high schools that were operational were Meadowlands High School and Sekano-Ntoane High School.

In March 1978 I went to boarding school in Herschel: Benson Mbeki High School. In June the students went on strike and students from the Transvaal were suspects. I was expelled. And so 1978 was another wasted year.

Perhaps 1979 was not entirely wasted, though it did not yield a matriculation qualification for Phydian Matsepe.

Phydian: In 1979 I taught as a private [part-time] teacher at Diepkloof Tsonga, renamed Diepdale High School. I went to class in 1980 and successfully completed matric at Orlando High School. In 1981 I was arrested and kept in solitary confinement for nine months. On my release I went to the Soweto College of Education where I studied for a teacher's diploma which I completed in 1984.

Bafana Hlatswayo also looks back to 1976 as the time when he first became politically aware. He had gained self-respect, but also gained a reputation as being a rebellious member of the 1976 generation.

Bafana: I gained a big thing [from] June 16th 1976. Today I am old enough – I know now how to talk to people, how to respect a person, how to fight for my rights. I think June 16th taught us a lot. We did not know that there was a person called Mandela. You could be arrested when you talked about that person, but June 16th taught us all those things which were concealed. So I think I am where I am because of June 16th.

[But] at various working places when they interview you, immediately when you talk about [Forms One,] Two, Three, they realise that you are the June 16th generation, and they don't employ you.

In addition he sees it as the beginning of his political education.

Bafana: After the release of Mandela things started to be mild, because everyone started to realise and feel that here is the person we were waiting for. I think he is our god. We were waiting for him on that day, the first time to see him, hear about him, his release, waiting for his date of release. I remember when I went to celebrate at FNB [Stadium] in 1990 where he was meeting the people of Soweto. I was so excited, it was about 15 000 or 29 000 people who were at FNB or 100 000! Really it was a jam-packing that day.

There are, however, some people who saw their involvement in the events of June 1976 as the point in their lives when their plans for the future derailed. Thomas Ntuli is a case in point. He had to abandon his plans for the future.

Thomas: I'm one of the victims. Ha, I told myself that I might become a lawyer. Because of '76 I was somewhat disturbed. Though I furthered my studies, but I was somewhat disturbed.

As I said, since we started the whole thing, that thing has affected me mentally, physically and spiritually. When I look at students today and I compare myself with them there is a different thing, it is a different thing. In fact somewhere a black youth's future was jeopardised, by June 16. Our generation, our future, was somewhere jeopardised. I don't blame the students, but I blame the government. Ja, I blame the government. Not exactly the government, but the system, they were using that time. Even now because we are still governed, but I am blaming the system. We used to call it 'the system', not the government.

I don't regret about this, because circumstances forced me to do this. I was forced. You know, when you're cornered, in a corner, you've got to fight for survival. When you're cornered, fight for survival.

Priscilla Msesenyane identified both positive and negative effects brought about by the events of 16 June 1976. She feels, however, that she had suffered mostly negative consequences of the uprising, whilst others who came after them reaped the benefits of their actions.

Priscilla: On the one hand it was wasted effort and time, yet it also had some good elements flowing from it. I was never able to concentrate on my schoolwork thereafter. Benefits flowed to other people.

Kedi Motsau's life was affected by the events of 16 June 1976. Not only did it interrupt her schooling and prevent her from completing her final examinations, but the involvement of her age group in the events — regardless of whether she had been an active participant or observer — stigmatised her and her fellow students as the troublemakers of 1976 and hampered their efforts to pursue their careers.

Kedi: Yes, it did affect me, because we couldn't write our exams, you couldn't learn. If you wanted to go back to school, the police were always there, there was nothing we could do. Until after two years, we managed to write our exams, but otherwise everything was interrupted. Besides that, if you want to get a job or something, they'd ask you … I went to Nelspruit and I wanted to do nursing, they asked me, 'Where are you from? Are you from Soweto? Now you bring that trouble.'

Even after we matriculated, we had these people who asked us if we are from Soweto, [from] all the corruption. We were labelled. Exactly, [labelled] as the troublemakers.

Like Priscilla Msesenyane, she also feels that the students who followed in their footsteps reaped the benefits of their actions. She reflects on the effects of 16 June 1976, and the four years it took for the then government to reverse the ruling on Afrikaans.

Kedi: Well, I would say that it was a terrible day, but that it was a good day, because we achieved what we wanted. Because they scrapped that Afrikaans as a medium of instruction. After it was scrapped, those students who were behind me were doing their mathematics in English. I said, 'Okay, it was worth it.'

Many of her friends went into exile; some joined Umkhonto we Sizwe and only returned after the elections in 1994. But Kedi did not consider going into exile as an alternative.

Kedi: It never crossed my mind to leave the country, because I didn't know what was there for me. So I never considered leaving the country, I was hoping things would be fine, and it's better to fight. It wasn't easy for us, for those who were left behind. It was not easy.

Joyce Makubele points to the stark contrasts between the actions of 16 June and the way in which the day is now celebrated.

Joyce: There was a lot of fighting on June 16. It brought a lot of changes. Now June 16 is a holiday. Before people were having their legs broken when they went to work.

The march into Johannesburg from Soweto on 22 September 1976 was a turning point for hundreds of students affected by the Soweto Revolt. The march, and the subsequent attack on Soweto residents by inmates from Mzimhlophe hostel, forced thousands of students to flee the country. Dingane Lebele remembers this time.

Dingane: After that march into town I never went back to school. If I went, it was not because I wanted to attend classes. I only went to attend meetings. I had already become militant. Many students were arrested during and after the march of 22 September 1976. So we demanded that they be released. It was then that I decided to flee the country and went to Botswana, becoming a political refugee.

Not all young men and women leaving the country at this stage were doing so because they were targeted by the security police. For some, it was pure adventure. Dingane Lebele's reason for leaving the country had much to do with the influence of peers who talked him into it.

Dingane: When I left the country, along with five of my friends, I was not 'hot', I was not on the police's wanted list. Victor Thamae came to us and suggested we leave the country to undergo military training. We just said yes! We started making arrangements and on 20th October 1976, the six of us were on our way to Botswana. In fact, we only became known to the security police after we had landed in Botswana. We never understood how the police came to know about our flight. However, we had reason to suspect that authorities in Botswana may have leaked the information to the South African security police.

Few of the students who left the country between September and December 1976 did so with the intention of obtaining a matriculation qualification. Many were eager to undergo military training and were immediately recruited by the African National Congress's military wing, Umkhonto we Sizwe. Dingane Lebele was one of them.

Dingane: When we arrived in Botswana we were kept in prison for three weeks. During the three weeks members of the Black Consciousness Movement came poaching us. They warned us about the dangers of joining the ANC, telling us that we would be 'sold' as others before us. They claimed that if we joined the Black Consciousness Movement, we would be given an opportunity to study in the United States and Europe. Some believed the stories. Me and my five companions insisted on talking to ANC representatives in Botswana.

For some, exile simply meant a continuation of the quest for education. These did not join the ANC, perceiving that the movement was only interested in making them into soldiers. Others saw membership of the ANC providing them with the opportunity to do what they had fled the country for – undergoing military training. By December 1976, some in the latter group were on their way to military camps in Tanzania. Dingane was happy to be among these.

Dingane: In December we were taken to Francis Town by the ANC representatives in Gaborone where we boarded a plane to Tanzania. By the end of the year we were in ANC camps in Tanzania, undergoing political education. We were taught about Karl Marx, Lenin, Ché Guevara and other prominent Socialists. We were even given the opportunity to read material by reactionaries like Mao Tse Tung and Trotsky.

At this stage some of those in Dingane's group, code-named 'the June 16 detachment' by the late Oliver Tambo, were re-thinking their commitment.

Dingane: A very militant member of our group, Ishmael 'Daddy' Chaka, became disillusioned. He complained that Lenin was becoming our 'new god' and that he did not like it. He was frequently away from the house, staying with Swahili friends he made in Dar-es-Salaam. When the June 16 detachment left Tanzania for basic military training in Angola in

April 1977, Chaka had left the camp permanently and was living in Dar-es-Salaam. He was an exceptional footballer and soon played for the local team.

Dingane values the training he received from the Cubans while in Angola between April and December 1977.

Dingane: The Cubans were very good. They gave excellent training in military hardware. Their classes were formal and conducted with discipline. But we learnt a lot more than any formal education system would have given us. At the end of the course in December we graduated. At this stage the detachment was broken up into groups and sent to the Soviet Union, Eastern Bloc and Cuba for advanced training. I was in the group heading for the Soviet Union.

Surrounded by South Africa, it was difficult for those seeking political refuge in Lesotho to undergo military training in 1976 and 1977. It was not until 1978, when the Chamber of Commerce in the Federal Republic of Germany offered scholarships to thousands of student exiles in southern Africa that many had an opportunity to leave the tiny kingdom.

But it was not the entire refugee community that took up the opportunity offered by the Germans. Some saw the offer as creating a diversion from the real challenges facing South Africans in exile. Steve Lebelo explains his point of view.

Steve: The fact that many among the student refugee community did not have matriculation qualification meant that they were going to be trained in carpentry, motor mechanics and building construction. Fields that did not really appeal to me. I stayed on and opted to try to obtain an 'A' level matriculation qualification. Barely two days after the massive departure of the refugee community for Germany, hundreds of students entered Lesotho from Bloemfontein, where there had been renewed student unrest in October 1978.

Scores of students fleeing police harassment in Bloemfontein entered Lesotho in large numbers in October 1978. Contending political organisations had an opportunity to lure new recruits after heavy losses occasioned by the opportunities of study offered by the Germans. However, many of the new intake of student refugees opted to group themselves in an ill-defined student organisation, hoping to forge links with the Soweto Student's Representative Council (SSRC) in exile in Botswana and Swaziland. Steve Lebelo, Oupa Mlangeni and Teboho Moremi formed the nucleus of this group.

Steve: The ANC in Lesotho was deprived of the opportunity to recruit students from Bloemfontein by the efforts of Oupa Mlangeni and Teboho Moremi who had already made contact with the contingency back in Bloemfontein. Mlangeni was Chairman of the Soweto Students' League (SSL) which tried to mobilise students briefly in Soweto in 1978. Police harassment forced them to flee to Bloemfontein, where they helped in the establishment of the Bloemfontein Students' League (BSL). After days of burning and looting in Bloemfontein, Mlangeni and Moremi were forced to flee the country into Lesotho in October 1978. On their trail were scores of students from Bloemfontein seeking political refuge in Lesotho.

Mlangeni saw himself as part of the SSRC and therefore aligned to the Black Consciousness Movement. Meeting Steve Lebelo gave him the opportunity to explore possibilities of reviving a student movement independent of the ANC and PAC.

Steve: All were received by me and hopes of reviving the students' movement in Lesotho, aligned to the Black Consciousness Movement, flared up again. I still continued with my quest for an 'A' level qualification while pursuing the long-term political aim. The new recruits from Bloemfontein briefly stayed at the refugee camp as was required by the Lesotho authorities. Shortly thereafter they sought accommodation outside the camp, coming to my place which I shared with Oupa Mlangeni and Teboho Moremi for meetings regularly.

Lebelo has a vivid recollection of the short history of the student exile movement in Lesotho.

Steve: With this new vitality brought by scores of new recruits from Bloemfontein and a few from Soweto, renewed commitment in the struggle set in. Once again, the desire to obtain an 'A' level qualification took the back seat. In March 1979 the SSRC in exile in Botswana, under Khotso Seathlolo's leadership, sent an envoy to Lesotho on a fact-finding mission. Arrangements were made for Oupa Mlangeni and me to attend a founding conference of the South African Youth Revolutionary Council (SAYRCO) in the Zambian capital of Lusaka during the Easter weekend of 1979. Obtaining travel documents as political refugees in Lesotho at this time was almost impossible. Delegates from Botswana, Swaziland and the United Kingdom attended the conference. In Lesotho we were denied the opportunity.

Soon after the Easter weekend of 1979 four delegates from the conference in Zambia arrived in Lesotho. Among them was Majakathata Mokwena, who had been elected publicity secretary of SAYRCO at the conference. The tempo of political activity in SAYRCO in Lesotho increased, distracting those who had returned to school.

Steve: Increased political activity left little time for serious study among the refugee student community in Lesotho. The commemoration of June 16 offered us the opportunity to announce our existence to the exiled movement. We immediately made it known that in 1979, the commemoration of the Soweto riots in Lesotho would be held under the auspices of SAYRCO. I was responsible for organising the event, and I was becoming less committed to my studies.

Between 1976 and 1979, the ANC dominated political activity in Lesotho, such as it was, among the exiled community. Political activity was confined to recruiting new refugees and organising commemoration services. The commemoration of the Soweto Revolt was a contested terrain. The ANC promoted a student movement at the University of Lesotho as the legitimate body to organise the commemoration service. Steve Lebelo explains the situation.

Steve: There was an emerging orthodoxy in Lesotho that the events of 16 June 1976 were orchestrated by ANC underground structures. This was contested by us in SAYRCO. The government of Lesotho recognised the ANC and to a lesser extent, the PAC. The battle for legitimacy in the organisation of the Soweto Revolt commemoration in 1979 was won by the ANC. This led to loss of confidence in SAYRCO.

173

Between June and end of August 1979, SAYRCO in Lesotho was ravaged by internal conflict. The leadership (including myself) was accused of bourgeois tendencies. By the end of August, nearly all the new recruits from the Bloemfontein Students' League, along with Teboho Moremi, had crossed the floor and joined the ANC.

Majakathata Mokwena left to further his studies at a university in the United Kingdom. Oupa Mlangeni lost interest in any political activity. I was nowhere near obtaining an 'A' level qualification. So by the end of 1979, I still did not have a matriculation qualification, and SAYRCO had ceased to exist.

Back in Soweto things were not any better for many who had chosen to stay behind and endure the 'system'. Hendrick Tshabalala, now disabled, also dreams of what might have been. Like many, he sees former President Nelson Mandela as his role model.

Hendrick: Hey man, it affected me a lot – especially educationally. Had it not been for June 16th, maybe I should have been someone like Mandela. Look, I have lost one leg and one hand. I started this staffriding in trains in 1976 when we were no longer schooling. It became a habit until I later got injured.

Unrest broke out in the Vaal area in 1984. Many students who had been in the lower levels of senior primary school, and who had not matriculated by then, were caught up in this unrest. Solomon Marikele went to Qwaqwa for two years, in an attempt to make progress educationally. In 1979 he returned to Soweto and enrolled at a nearby school early in 1980. Inevitably, Solomon was caught up in the events that broke out on 3 September 1984, while he was a student. He again relished the role of arch arsonist.

Solomon: I continued with this thing up until 1984, where we again crashed bottle stores with buses. We just approached the bus driver and said: 'Hey baba, out!'

You take the bus, you reverse that thing, you crash that thing, it falls down. We take all the liquor, we go back to school again. You get drunk. We start to trouble the mayors until the mayors ran away from Soweto. The government have given them the place in Fordsburg, they stayed

174

there, others stay in Power Park, there next to the power station, electrical power station.

The way those leaders used to tell us and say: 'Hey guys, it's not a fun, it's a really thing, we make it and one day we will survive.'

So it was not a fun. We were really angry for what was happening to us at school. So we joined the march ...

Although Solomon was never arrested, he soon became aware that the police were looking for him, and friends came to warn him.

Solomon: They said: 'Hey buddy, watch out, these guys they've got names of those who are leading the crew, so you must be careful.'

So I told my mom: 'Mom, I am a leader, so take me somewhere to hide.'

My mom took me there to Qwaqwa one or two years. I came back in 1979 when I remember [I was] schooling again.

He did not however, relinquish his participation in the struggle and increasingly leaned towards criminal activity. In the 1980s he started on a life of crime.

Solomon: It started settling down in 1986. I said, no fuck, I've fought a lot, so let me relax. Let me do the other things.

We started saying: 'Let's now start to repossess.'

Mostly the students of 1984, '85, we said: 'Now gents, now we repossess, we can't drive horses now. This is a new country, we have to drive cars.'

We know a white man can go and buy things like that. Others they do housebreaking, others they do bank robberies, it was group by group.

Others followed in his wake.

Solomon: Mostly those who are there, they were students. So they saw they can't go further with education and now they have to repossess, there is nothing we can do, we need to survive. This is our country, so we have to take anything from them, bring [it] to us. They've got money, we've got nothing. They will buy and we will steal, just like that, you know. We change hands. They know we live just like that.

I'm proud, I am really proud, because now things are coming really, really the right way.

175

Finally, parents were deeply affected by the death of their children during the uprising. For many, it led to a total transformation of the lives of surviving relatives. The loss of her son has left an indelible impression on Susan Ndlovu.

'I will comment on the death of my son,' says Susan. 'It is said that my son died for June 16. As a parent, I wanted to know if my son broke any law. When I discovered that he was killed, I laid a charge and tried to claim compensation from the State. Yet the case just ended inconclusively. They said I have won. Won what? He left two young children. To date I am struggling with them. They have not had a decent education. I could not afford to give them a decent education. They only reached Standard Five (Grade Seven). Even then, they struggled to get there.'

But Susan is comforted by the subsequent political developments.

'We thought our children were doing something right,' she says. 'Since then, we have been able to communicate better with white people. Before then, there was no communication between us and white people. We were subservient and docile. The children helped us and we were able to communicate with white people.'

4

5

1. 1976: This beer hall suffered extensive damage during the uprising. From late afternoon on 16 June 1976, students attacked and looted beer halls, liquor stores and bar-lounges and took the looted alcohol home. Some were reprimanded by their elders and one youngster was even told to return his loot – an impossible task, given the situation in the streets. Photo: *Rapport*

2. 1976: An unidentified shop-owner stands amidst the ruins of what used to be his shop before it was destroyed. The anger of the students was not only turned on whites; at times their frustration was also vented on the adults in their own community. Photo: *Rapport*

3. 1976; A few people cluster in front of plain-clothes policemen. After 16 June people in the townships became used to the presence of police and soldiers in the streets, at their homes and at sports meetings. Soweto found itself virtually under martial law and in a state of occupation. Photo: *City Press*

4. Intense discussions at a meeting in one of the destroyed Soweto schools in early 1977. Students whose schooling had been abruptly terminated in June 1976 attempted to return to school, only to find that classrooms had been destroyed and that studying was all but impossible. Photo: *Rapport*

5. 1976: 'Nkosi Sikelel' iAfrika' featured prominently as one of the freedom songs sang on 16 June. Members of the white community showed their solidarity with the Soweto uprising using this song, a song which was to play an important role in the political struggle of the late seventies and eighties, and which was elevated to democratic South Africa's new national anthem in 1994. Photo: MuseuMAfrica

SUE KRIGE

During most of the twentieth century in South Africa the government ran segregated schools for whites, Coloureds and Indians, but allocated whites the main share of resources. Until 1953 black children only had access to education through schools run by various mission organisations in what historians call the 'mission school system'. From the mid-nineteenth century church missionary societies ran almost all schools for Africans, and the government paid only for teachers' salaries. However, there were not enough mission schools to cater for more than a small number of African children. By the 1940s, only 25 per cent of African children of school-going age actually went to school, and the mission system was in a state of collapse. In spite of this, many future black leaders in South Africa were trained at these mission schools. They included the leaders of the African National Congress (ANC) such as Nelson Mandela and Oliver Tambo, and Robert Sobukwe of the Pan African Congress (PAC).

When the National Party came to power in 1948, it ordered an investigation of African or ' Bantu' education, as it was known. The result was a law passed in 1953 which removed African education from the control of the missionaries and instituted a four-year, state-controlled junior primary curriculum. This curriculum was designed to incorporate the ideas of National Party educationalists about the future role, needs and culture of the 'Bantu', as black people were then called. It extended this 'Bantu Education' to thousands of black children all over South Africa, particularly in the urban areas such as Soweto.

In the early fifties, as part of a broader anti-apartheid Defiance Campaign, ANC leaders and parents tried to resist what they called the newly instituted 'gutter education' and even formed alternative schools. However, the police harassed and arrested parents and teachers to the extent that they were not able to compete with the offer of free (but not com-

179

pulsory) state schooling for black children, where previously there had been very few opportunities for education.

During the late 1950s education issues were overshadowed by political developments. In 1956 most of the anti-apartheid leaders of all races were arrested and put on trial for treason, a process which lasted until early 1960 when the PAC and ANC were banned. After the Rivonia Trial in 1963, Nelson Mandela and most of the leaders of the ANC were found guilty of treason and sentenced to life imprisonment. During the remainder of the 1960s, the government made sure that all black junior secondary (Grades Eight to Ten) and senior secondary schools (Grades Eleven and Twelve), as well as ethnically based teacher training colleges and universities, were confined to the newly established 'Bantu homelands', predominantly rural areas based on the old 'native reserves'. These homelands, 13 per cent of the land, were far removed from the rapidly increasing numbers of urban students who were passing through the education system and aspired to access to matriculation level.

Why did the uprising start in Soweto? And why did it take place in June 1976? Historians talk about the period of the 1960s as a time of massive oppression where leaders were banned, were in prison or in exile. They also note major negative socio-economic changes, the emergence of new ideologies of resistance and the decolonisation of neighbouring African states.

In education the government clamped down on protests organised by parents and teachers, and used the homeland system to enforce influx control, and to deal with troublemakers. There were only small sporadic incidents of resistance in a number of schools that had originally been mission schools.

However, by the late 1960s and early 1970s the context was changing. There were major socio-economic changes in which the slowing down of the economy led to pressure from business groups to extend secondary schooling for black youths in the urban areas. More black people were needed who could become semi-skilled workers in previously 'white' jobs. The government bowed to the pressure and abandoned its previous policy of restricting post-primary schooling for black students to the homelands. From the early 1970s it expanded state schooling in urban townships, particularly Soweto. A total of 40 new schools were built in the sprawling township. Here, secondary students crowded together in new classrooms with few resources and under- or unqualified teachers. On a higher level, school boards, which were supposed to represent the government and parents, kept an eye on troublesome, politically aware teachers and students.

As the economic downturn continued, however, graduates of the newly established schools, particularly in Soweto, found that there were very few jobs available. They became angry, despairing and frustrated. A new generation of very young, politically conscious black youth established itself by 1974. It criticised older parents, teachers and ministers of religion for their inability to act against Bantu Education and oppressive apartheid measures in general.

In addition, some of the younger teachers, also in Soweto, had come from the ethnically divided campuses of Fort Hare and the University of the North, where they had formed the South African Student's Organisation (SASO). The organisation was based on the philosophy of Black Consciousness and was associated with Steve Biko. These young professionals had a major impact on emerging student organisations such as the South African Student's Movement (SASM), which were founded in schools. Some accounts even refer to SASM as a school-based branch of SASO. Statements by SASM and SASO reflected the growing excitement felt by young black people, inspired by the workers' strikes of 1973 in Durban, the fall of the Portuguese regimes in Angola and Mozambique in 1975, and the successes of resistance movements in the war in Rhodesia.

In mid-1974 the Department of Bantu Education decided to do two things that ultimately drove students to protest. It doubled the numbers of pupils going from primary schools into Standard Six (Grade Eight) at junior secondary schools without making provision for these students. There were not enough classrooms, not enough teachers, not enough learning materials. The department also announced that it would enforce a provision, made in 1953, that students would have to learn half their subjects in English and the other half (including Maths, History and Biology) through the medium of Afrikaans. School boards petitioned the Department of Bantu Education, and when this failed, some members resigned *en masse*.

From about May 1976, students themselves began to protest against the Afrikaans decree by boycotting classes, by not allowing teachers to teach in Afrikaans, and by burning Afrikaans books and test papers. One of the centres was Phefeni Junior Secondary School in Orlando West. SASM began to organise formal meetings at schools like Morris Isaacson High School, Naledi Secondary School and Phefeni Junior Secondary School. Inspectors told teachers at meetings to follow the decree or lose their jobs. Teachers began to leave the profession. Well-known personalities like Percy Qoboza, editor of *The World*, and Helen Suzman, the lone anti-apartheid crusader in parliament, met with the Minister of Bantu Education, but without success. After canvassing schools, on 13 June 1976, student leaders from SASM held a meeting in Orlando East to plan a protest march for the 16th. It would start from various points in Soweto and end at Orlando Stadium, also in Orlando East.

Biographical details of respondents at the time of the interviews in 2001

'BAFANA'

'DAN'

Surname: Hlatswayo
Name(s): Bafana
Date of birth: 7 July 1965
Place of birth: Dhlamini 2
Father's occupation: Tank engineer
Mother's occupation: Worked for Dorian Knitting Company
Sibling(s): Three brothers and two sisters
Who else lived in the house? No one
First moved to Soweto? Born in Soweto
In which part (of Soweto) did you live? Dhlamini 2
Schooling
Junior Primary: Nonto
Senior Primary: Ndondo
Junior Secondary: Ibhongo
Senior Secondary: Ibhongo
School on 16 June 1976: Nonto
Grade in 1976: Grade 5
Grade completed: Grade 12
Present job: Merchandising
Living conditions in 1976: 'Together with my brothers I slept in the dining room, whereas my sisters used the small bedroom.'

Surname: Moyane
Name(s): Dan Tsakani
Date of birth: 9 March 1959
Place of birth: Johannesburg
Father's occupation: Worked as a labourer
Mother's occupation: Worked in a crèche
Sibling(s): One sister (Ellen); no brothers
Who else lived in the house? No one
First moved to Soweto? Born there
In which part (of Soweto) did you live? White City Jabavu
Schooling
Junior Primary: Vukani
Senior Primary: Eiselen
Junior Secondary: Molapo
Senior Secondary: Morris Isaacson High
School on 16 June 1976: Morris Isaacson High
Grade in 1976: Grade 11
Grade completed: Grade 12
Present job: Station manager, Radio 702
Living conditions in 1976: 'I slept on a sofa in the dining room. My sister slept on the floor in my parents' bedroom. If we had visitors, I slept on the floor.'

'DIKELEDI'

Surname: Motswene

Name(s): Dikeledi Johannah

Date of birth: 27 April 1963

Place of birth: Alexandra

Father's occupation: Pherebe (a policeman) in Alexandra

Mother's occupation: Domestic worker
in Sandton

Sibling(s): Four brothers; two sisters

Who else lived in the house? Makaphifo,
a family helper

First moved to Soweto? 1969

In which part (of Soweto) did you live?
Dube

Schooling

Junior Primary: Mfundisweni

Senior Primary: Mfundisweni

Junior Secondary: Ithute

Senior Secondary: Ithute

School on 16 June 1976: Ithute (later
Alexandra High)

Grade in 1976: Grade 9

Grade completed: Grade 12

Present job: Hospital worker

Living conditions in 1976: 'My sister
and I were boarders with a family in
Dube, but schooled in Alexandra
township on the other side of Johannesburg. We slept on the kitchen floor
not to disturb the family.'

'DINGANE'

Surname: Lebele

Name(s): Dingane

Date of birth: 1958

Place of birth: Alexandra

Father's occupation: Died when he was
very young – he knows very little
about his father

Mother's occupation: Domestic worker
in Yeoville

Sibling(s): Three brothers; no sisters

Who else lived in the house? 'Many
relatives had their own houses in the
yard but they did not live in the
house.'

First moved to Soweto? 1964

In which part (of Soweto) did you live?
Diepkloof

Schooling

Junior Primary: Alexandra and Ikaneng

Senior Primary: Tlotlego

Junior Secondary: Lofentse

Senior Secondary: Madibane

School on 16 June 1976: Madibane

Grade in 1976: Grade 9

Grade completed: Matric. Has a B.Sc. in
Engineering

Present job: Major, South African Airforce

Living conditions in 1976: 'Two boys
shared the dining room and the others
shared the small bedroom.'

184

'ERIC'

Surname: Nkuna
Name(s): Eric
Date of birth: 4 March 1965
Place of birth: Chiawelo, Soweto
Father's occupation: Worked for
  Chemoplus
Mother's occupation: Housewife
Sibling(s): Two brothers; one sister
Who else lived in the house? 'So many,
  mostly relatives who were our tenants,
  at times we had two extra families. I
  can't remember exactly, but there could
  have been more than 15 in the house.'
First moved to Soweto? Born in Soweto
In which part (of Soweto) did you live?
  Chiawelo
Schooling
Junior Primary: St Matthews Roman
  Catholic School
Senior Primary: St Matthews Roman
  Catholic School
Junior Secondary: Never attended
Senior Secondary: Never attended
School on 16 June 1976: St Matthews
Grade in 16: Grade 5
Grade completed: Grade 4
Present job: Machine operator, Nampak
Living conditions in 1976: 'Sometimes
  we could share the dinning room, being
  seven or eight, whereas my sister and
  the other female tenants' children
  shared the kitchen, being five or six.'

'GANDHI'

Surname: Malungane
Name(s): Rodgers Gandhi
Date of birth: 7 June 1964
Place of birth: Old Pimville
Father's occupation: Worked for
  National Clothing
Mother's occupation: Housewife
Sibling(s): Six brothers; three sisters
Who else lived in the house? 'Besides
  my family there was my uncle and
  family who were five in number.'
First moved to Soweto? 'At a tender age.'
In which part (of Soweto) did you live?
  Chiawelo 1
Schooling
Junior Primary: Tiakeni
Senior Primary: Basani
Junior Secondary: Nghungunyane
Senior Secondary: Sekano-Ntoane and
  Mawhawha
School on 16 June 1976: Nghungunyane
Grade in 1976: Grade 8
Grade completed: Grade 12
Present job: Researcher
Living conditions in 1976: 'I slept in the
  kitchen with some of my siblings.'

'GEORGE'

Surname: Baloyi
Name(s): George
Date of birth: 27 June 1957
Place of birth: Chiawelo, Soweto
Father's occupation: Major in the SADF
  21 battalion, fought in World War II
Mother's occupation: Housewife
Sibling(s): Four brothers; three sisters
Who else lived in the house? No one
First moved to Soweto? Born in Soweto
In which part (of Soweto) did you live?
  Chiawelo
Schooling
Junior Primary: Tiakeni
Senior Primary: Gazankulu
Junior Secondary: Nghungunyane
Senior Secondary: Never attended
School on 16 June 1976: Nghunguynane
Grade in 1976: Grade 9
Grade completed: Grade 9
Present job: Driver for a stationery
  company
Living conditions in 1976: 'My sisters
  slept in the small bedroom and all the
  boys slept in the dining room.
  Porridge and a variety of relish, egg,
  meat, cabbage, was our everyday
  ration.'

'HENDRICK'

Surname: Tshabalala
Name(s): Hendrick Tugoe
Date of birth: 6 June 1963
Place of birth: Midway (Chiawelo 2)
Father's occupation: Radio mechanic,
  Sharp (Pty) Ltd, in Jeppe
Mother's occupation: Can't remember
  where she worked
Sibling(s): Five brothers; four sisters
Who else lived in the house? No one
First moved to Soweto? Born in Soweto
In which part (of Soweto) did you live?
  Midway (Chiawelo 2)
Schooling
Junior Primary: Hitekani
Senior Primary: Gazankulu
Junior Secondary: Vuwani
Senior Secondary: Never attended
School on 16 June 1976: Gazankulu
Grade in 1976: Grade 5
Grade completed: Grade 11
Present job: Motor mechanic
Living conditions in 1976: 'Ja, we slept
  very nice, especially when my siblings
  left the house. But before they left there
  was one room for them, my sisters,
  whereas I myself was in the dining room
  with all those who come after me. My
  father was earning enough to maintain
  us, we enjoyed ourselves. The problem
  was solved when one of my brothers
  got a job and left the house, and my
  sister got married.'

'ERICK'

Surname: Ngobeni
Name(s): Joseph Erick
Date of birth: 17 April 1964
Place of birth: Old Pimville
Father's occupation: Unknown
Mother's occupation: Unknown
Sibling(s):
Who else lived in the house? No one
First moved to Soweto? 'At a very young age.'
In which part (of Soweto) did you live? Dhlamini

Schooling

Junior Primary: Emadlelweni
Senior Primary: Hlakaniphani
Junior Secondary: Never attended
Senior Secondary: Never attended
School on 16 June 1976: Hlakaniphani
Grade in 1976: Grade 7
Grade completed: Grade 6
Present job: Street hawker

'JOYCE'

Surname: Makhubele
Name(s): Joyce Khobeni
Date of birth: 15 October 1965
Place of birth: Baragwanath Hospital (Chiawelo)
Father's occupation: Municipal policeman
Mother's occupation: Housewife
Sibling(s): Two brothers and three sisters
Who else lived in the house? Two cousins and their wives
First moved to Soweto? Born in Soweto
In which part (of Soweto) did you live? Chiawelo

Schooling

Junior Primary: Tiakeni
Senior Primary: Mapelong (Northern Province)
Junior Secondary: Never attended
School on 16 June 1976: Tiakeni
Grade in 1976: Sub A
Grade completed: Grade 9
Present job: Unemployed
Living conditions in 1976: 'My cousin with his spouse slept in the small bedroom whereas the other cousin also with his wife slept in the dining room. All of us shared the bedroom with our parents. Porridge and offal was our daily food.'

187

'KEDI'

Surname: Motsau
Name(s): Naledi Kedi
Date of birth: 1955
Place of birth: Alexandra
Father's occupation: Worker
Mother's occupation: Worker
Sibling(s): Two brothers
Who else lived in the house? Two cousins
First moved to Soweto? 1972
In which part (of Soweto) did you live?
  Naledi
Schooling
Junior Primary: Ikage
Senior Primary: Ithute
Junior Secondary: Naledi High
Senior Secondary: Naledi High
School on 16 June 1976: Naledi High
Grade in 1976: Grade 12
Grade completed: Grade 12
Present job: Worker, Northern
  Metropolitan Local Council
Living conditions in 1976: 'Boys slept in
  the dining room whereas all girls slept
  in the small bedroom.'

'MARTHA'

Surname: Matthews
Name(s): Martha Mabel
Date of birth: 11 September 1954
Place of birth: Alexandra
Father's occupation: Factory worker in
  Croesus
Mother's occupation: Dressmaker and a
  woman priest
Sibling(s): Two brothers; three sisters
Who else lived in the house? No one
First moved to Soweto? 'When I was a
  few months old.'
In which part (of Soweto) did you live?
  Meadowlands Zone 7
Schooling
Junior Primary: Nkwe
Senior Primary: Tswelelang
Junior Secondary: Kelekitso
Senior Secondary: Kelekitso
School on 16 June 1976: Kelekitso
Grade completed: Grade 12
Living conditions in 1976: 'When we
  grew up we mixed ourselves together
  i.e. my father and mother in one room
  and then the rest of us slept in one
  room – until such time when [we]
  noticed that there was a difference
  between a male and a female! Then
  the boys slept in the dining room
  while the girls slept in the bedroom.
  My parents' income was not satisfying
  because at the end of the day you
  could not find the exact thing you
  wanted.'

'MUZIKAYISE'

Surname: Ntuli
Name(s): Muzikayise
Place of birth: Dhlamini 1
Father's occupation: Municipal office
 worker, Senaoane
Mother's occupation: Hawker
Sibling(s): Three brothers
Who else lived in the house? No one
In which part (of Soweto) did you live?
 Dhlamini 1
Schooling
Junior Primary: St Matthews Roman
 Catholic School
Senior Primary: St Matthews Roman
 Catholic School
Junior Secondary: Senaoane
Senior Secondary: Never attended
School on 16 June 1976: St Matthews
 Roman Catholic
Grade in 1976: Grade 8
Grade completed: Grade 9
Present job: Unemployed
Living conditions in 1976: 'We slept in
 the dining room together with my
 younger brothers whereas the elder
 brother slept in the small bedroom.'

'PHYDIAN'

Surname: Matsepe
Name(s): Phydian Mantsho Smadzadza
Date of birth: 12 December 1959
Place of birth: Sophiatown
Father's occupation: Passed away while
 he was an infant
Mother's occupation: Housewife
Sibling(s): Two brothers; one sister
Who else lived in the house? No one
First moved to Soweto? 1959
In which part (of Soweto) did you live?
 Diepkloof
Schooling
Junior Primary: Ditawana
Senior Primary: Ditau
Junior Secondary: Orlando High/Benson
 Mbeki
Senior Secondary: Orlando High
 School/Benson Mbeki
School on 16 June 1976: Orlando High
Grade in 1976: Grade 11
Present job: Minister, Methodist Church
Living conditions in 1976: 'The parents
 used one bedroom and the girls used
 the other bedroom. We boys slept in
 the dining room. In winter we slept in
 the kitchen because it was warm.'

 'PRISCILLA'

Surname: Msesenyane
Name(s): Priscilla
Date of birth: 27 December 1965
Place of birth: Chiawelo
Father's occupation: Worked for the
  Steyn Brothers Co.
Mother's occupation: Worked for Pick 'n
  Pay
Sibling(s): One brother; one sister
Who else lived in the house? No one
In which part (of Soweto) did you live?
  Chiawelo
Schooling
Junior Primary: St Matthews Roman
  Catholic School
Senior Primary: St Matthews Roman
  Catholic School
Junior Secondary: Senaoane
Senior Secondary: Never attended
School on 16 June 1976: St Matthews
Grade in 1976: Grade 4
Grade completed: Grade 9
Present job: Unemployed
Living conditions in 1976: 'We shared
  the small bedroom with my brother
  until he decided to occupy the dining
  room after he felt like he was old
  enough. We ate a variety of reasonable
  food.'

 'SAM'

Surname: Khoza
Name(s): Sam Pikane
Date of birth: 14 July 1963
Place of birth: Chiawelo
Father's occupation: Self
  employed/Merchant
Mother's occupation:
  Housewife/Merchant
Sibling(s): Five brothers; three sisters
Who else lived in the house? No one
First moved to Soweto? Born in Soweto
In which part (of Soweto) did you live?
  Chiawelo
Schooling
Junior Primary: Inkwenzeni (Nelspruit)
Senior Primary: Inkwenzeni
Junior Secondary: Ibhongo
Senior Secondary: Ibhongo
School on 16 June 1976: Ibhongo
Grade in 1976: Grade 10
Grade completed: Grade 11
Present job: Self employed
Living conditions in 1976: 'My sisters
  slept in a dining room, my brother
  and his wife occupied the small bed-
  room while I slept in the kitchen
  together with my other brothers.'

'SAM'

Surname: Zikhali
Name(s): Sam Thami
Date of birth: 6 October 1963
Place of birth: Emdeni
Father's occupation: Worked as a driver
  for various companies
Mother's occupation: Unknown
Sibling(s): Three brothers; two sisters
Who else lived in the house? No one
First moved to Soweto? Born in Soweto
In which part (of Soweto) did you live?
  Dhlamini 1
Schooling
Junior Primary: Isipho Community
Senior Primary: Emadlelweni Senior
  and Dlambulo
Junior Secondary: Ibhongo
Senior Secondary: Ibhongo
School on 16 June 1976: Ibhongo
Grade in 1976: Grade 8
Grade completed: Grade 12
Present job: Worker, Northern
  Metropolitan Local Council
Living conditions in 1976: 'We were not
  a big family, we were four boys and two
  girls. Two young girls were born in
  Dhlamini and so that means at Emndeni
  we were young. We slept in one room,
  all four boys, and the parents in the
  other room. It was a four-roomed house,
  then we shifted to Dhlamini and the
  family grew up to six children. They
  built two rooms and a garage so there
  were a lot of space for us to share.'

'SOLLY'

Surname: Mpshe
Name(s): Solomon Ramogale
Date of birth: 1958
Place of birth: Orlando East, Soweto
Father's occupation: Worked as a security
  man for a furniture company
Mother's occupation: Factory worker in
  the garment industry, Doornfontein
Sibling(s): Three brothers; one sister
Who else lived in the house? No one
First moved to Soweto? Born in Soweto
In which part (of Soweto) did you live?
  Tladi
Schooling
Junior Primary: Orlando East
Senior Primary: Taupele
Junior Secondary: Moletsane
Senior Secondary: Morris Isaacson
School on 16 June 1976: Morris Isaacson
  High
Grade in 1976: Grade 10
Grade completed: Grade 12
Present job: Works at Standard Bank
  Headquarters
Living conditions in 1976: 'We were for-
  tunate to have two bedrooms. The one
  was for the kids and the other one was
  for my parents. Our sister had to sleep
  in the dining room because she was a
  girl. But otherwise we had two beds
  in our bedroom and as the oldest I was
  fortunate to have my three-quarter-size
  bed and the others were using the
  other bed. With their income they were
  able to ensure that there was always
  food.'

191

'SOLOMON'

Surname: Marikele
Name(s): Solomon
Place of birth: Chiawelo, Soweto
Father's occupation: Worked in the Eskom head office
Mother's occupation: Worked for Anglo-American Ltd, Braamfontein
Sibling(s): One brother; two sisters
Who else lived in the house? No one
First moved to Soweto? Born in Soweto
In which part (of Soweto) did you live? Chiawelo

Schooling

Junior Primary: Tiakeni
Senior Primary: Rhulane
Junior Secondary: Nghungunyane
Senior Secondary: Sekano-Ntoane
School on 16 June 1976: Rhulane
Grade in 1976: Grade 4
Grade completed: Grade 10
Present job: Unemployed
Living conditions in 1976: 'I and my brothers slept in the dining room whereas my sisters used the small bedroom.'

'STEVE'

Surname: Lebelo
Name(s): Malesela Steve
Date of birth: 27 June 1958
Place of birth: Orlando, Soweto
Father's occupation: Self employed as coal and wood merchant
Mother's occupation: Housewife
Sibling(s): Three brothers; two sisters
Who else lived in the house? No one
First moved to Soweto? Born in Soweto
In which part (of Soweto) did you live? Diepkloof

Schooling

Junior Primary: Bonega
Senior Primary: Qhoboshaeane
Junior Secondary: Qhoboshaeane
Senior Secondary: Madibane High
School on 16 June 1976: Madibane High
Grade in 1976: Grade 12
Grade completed: Grade 12
Present job: Wits Foundation, University of the Witwatersrand
Living conditions in 1976: 'People, they actually grow, for instance when I was twelve, that could have been 1970 I was twelve, my eldest brother could have been 25, 26. That would mean that we can't be in the same bedroom, and that is when the dining room came in handy. During the day it would serve the purpose of a dining room, but at night it would then double as a bedroom, because we had to be separated when we were older, but usually yes we would all be in the bedroom and my parents would be in the other bedroom.'

'THAILANE'

Surname: Ngobeni
Name(s): Thailane
Date of birth: 14 July1957
Place of birth: Chiawelo, Soweto
Father's occupation: Unknown
Mother's occupation: Worked in Pensioners' Administration Department
Sibling(s): Eight half-brothers; one half-sister
Who else lived in the house? At times about twelve people, including half brothers and sisters
First moved to Soweto? Born in Soweto
In which part (of Soweto) did you live? Chiawelo

Schooling

Junior Primary: Tiakeni
Senior Primary: Basani and Gazankulu
Junior Secondary: Nghungunyane
Senior Secondary: Never attended
School on 16 June 1976: Nghungunyane
Grade in 1976: Grade 10
Grade completed: Grade 9
Present job: Corporal
Living conditions in 1976: 'I slept in the dining room while my sisters slept in the small bedroom. We used to eat dry porridge with raw tomato as a relish, finish and klaar.'

'THOMAS'

Surname: Ntuli
Name(s): Thomas
Date of birth: 6 April 1962
Place of birth: Old Pimville
Father's occupation: Died when he was two years old – he knows very little about his father
Mother's occupation: Sold vegetables (only family income)
Sibling(s): One brother; three sisters
Who else lived in the house? No one
First moved to Soweto? 'When I was a few months old.'
In which part (of Soweto) did you live? Chiawelo

Schooling

Junior Primary: Tiakeni
Senior Primary: Basani
Junior Secondary: Nghungunyane
Senior Secondary: Nghungunyane
Grade in 1976: Grade 8
Grade completed: Grade 10
Present job: Unemployed
Living conditions in 1976: 'Oh, sleeping conditions, it was fine, because it was just our family and nobody else. I never had my breakfast before I went to school because Nghungunyane was nearer to my place. I just run home, have two slices of bread and drink tea, black tea.'

'TONY'

Surname: Hanyane
Name(s): Tony
Date of birth: 9 November 1969
Place of birth: Chiawelo
Father's occupation: Worked in the His
  Majesty's Building
Mother's occupation: Nurse
Sibling(s): Three brothers; one sister
Who else lived in the house? Aunt
First moved to Soweto? Born in Soweto
In which part (of Soweto) did you live?
  Chiawelo
Schooling
Junior Primary: Tiakeni
Senior Primary: Rhulane
Junior Secondary: Sekano/Shingwedzi
Senior Secondary: Sekano/Shingwedzi
School on 16 June 1976: Tiakeni
Grade in 1976: Grade 5
Grade completed: Grade 12
Present job: Unemployed
Living conditions in 1976: 'We slept
  together in the dining room.'

'TULU'

Surname: Mhlanga
Name(s): Bafana Tulu
Date of birth: 10 September 1965
Place of birth: Chiawelo, Soweto
Father's occupation: Factory worker in
  Johannesburg
Mother's occupation: Housewife
Sibling(s): Five brothers; no sisters
Who else lived in the house? No one
First moved to Soweto? Born in Soweto
In which part (of Soweto) did you live?
  Chiawelo
Schooling
Junior Primary: Tiakeni
Senior Primary: Gazankulu
Junior Secondary: Progress (Pimville)
Senior Secondary: Never attended
School on 16 June 1976: Tiakeni
Grade in 1976: Grade 3
Grade completed: Grade 8
Present job: Self employed (motor
  mechanic)
Living conditions in 1976: 'I slept in the
  dining room. My two elder brothers
  slept in the small bedroom as the rest
  of us used the dining room.'

'VICTOR'

Surname: Buthelezi
Name(s): Dumisani Victor
Date of birth: 30 September 1964
Place of birth: Dhlamini 1, Soweto
Father's occupation: Worked for various companies around Johannesburg
Mother's occupation: Domestic worker
Sibling(s): One brother; one sister
Who else lived in the house?
First moved to Soweto? Born in Soweto
In which part (of Soweto) did you live? Dhlamini 1

Schooling

Junior Primary: Hlakaniphani
Senior Primary: Lilydale
Junior Secondary: Ibhongo
Senior Secondary: Fort Louis and Nghungunyane
School on 16 June 1976: Lilydale
Grade in 1976: Grade 6
Grade completed: Grade 11
Present Job: Unemployed
Living conditions in 1976: 'I slept in the dining room whereas my sister slept in the small bedroom and my younger brother slept with my parents in the main bedroom.'

'VICTOR'

Surname: Kubayi
Name(s): Victor
Date of birth: 3 July 1964
Place of birth: Chiawelo
Father's occupation: Worked for Naschem
Mother's occupation: Worked in Mariston Hotel
Sibling(s): Four brothers; one sister
Who else lived in the house? No one
First moved to Soweto? Born in Soweto
In which part (of Soweto) did you live? Chiawelo

Schooling

Junior Primary: Tiakeni
Senior Primary: Rhulane
Junior Secondary: Vuwani
Senior Secondary: Vuwani
Grade in 1976: Grade 2
Grade completed: Grade 12
Present job: Jeweller
Living conditions in 1976: 'Four boys slept in the small bedroom while the other brother who was young then slept with my parents in the main bedroom. My sister was not yet born.'

 'VUSI'

Surname: Zwane
Name(s): Vusi Sipho
Date of birth: 19 November 1962
Place of birth: White City, Soweto
Father's occupation: Worked for
    Schindler
Mother's occupation: Domestic worker
Sibling(s): Two brothers; six sisters
Who else lived in the house? No one
First moved to Soweto? Born in Soweto
In which part (of Soweto) did you live?
    Chiawelo
Schooling
Junior Primary: Tiakeni
Senior Primary: Rhulane
Junior Secondary: Nghungunyane
Senior Secondary: Vuwani
School on June 16: Rhulane
Grade in 1976: Grade 5
Grade completed: Grade 12
Present job: Unemployed
Living conditions in 1976: 'I slept in a
    small bedroom whereas my two
    brothers slept in the dining room. My
    sisters stayed with my parents.'

Why this book was written
Notes from the authors

ELSABÉ BRINK

On 16 June 1976 I was a rookie language teacher at a high school, safely tucked away in the city bowl of Cape Town. My only link to the events unfolding in Soweto was through the media: newspapers, radio news and occasional viewing of the news broadcasts on the brand new SABC-TV.

We were, however, not untouched by the unfolding events. At the time a senior history teacher, during a discussion in the staffroom, planted himself in front of me, towered over me, shook his finger 'Groot Krokodil'-style, and asserted that it was me and my liberalisms that had caused all these troubles. In later years, as I studied history at university, I came across descriptions and analyses of the events in the standard reference works on South African history. But these events remained far removed, the stuff history books are made of.

In 1999 I was asked by the National Monuments Council (now the South African Heritage Resource Agency) to look for, identify and research the history of some fifty sites of historical interest in Soweto. This was done with the help of a research team consisting of six colleagues who were all born and bred in Soweto. The assignment led us on a voyage of discovery into the historical heart of Soweto. We started off by listing the obvious places of interest, almost all political in nature, which are most often visited by tourists to Soweto. These include Freedom Square in Kliptown where the Freedom Charter was drafted in 1955, the Regina Mundi Catholic Church, Baragwanath Hospital, the Mandela Museum and the Hector Peterson monument in Orlando West.

As a matter of priority we also investigated the route followed by students during the 1976 Soweto uprising. We wanted to know exactly where the students gathered and marched after they had left Morris Isaacson High School, and where other groups of students, such as those who came by train from the far west of Soweto, had joined them.

As our research progressed, the information gathered became more complex and more questions emerged. Steve Lebelo, a member of the team, began to relate his experiences in Diepkloof on 16 June 1976. We realised that the march from Morris Isaacson to Orlando West was not the only march that took place on that day. There were other marches, but no one had documented these. Who could tell us about events which occurred on that day in Meadowlands north of the railway line, Orlando East, Pimville, Chiawelo, Naledi, Klipspruit? Each member of the team had another story to relate, of how he or she had seen a bottle store being burnt down, or how the schoolchildren had turned around and left the school premises just after assembly with the teachers being unable to prevent the exodus, knowing what was about to happen.

One day Steve told me about his brother, Abe, who was killed on the ill-fated march of 4 August 1976. Abe was 20 years old when he died. Steve related how 1976 had disrupted his life, how he had gone into exile and had spent three years in Lesotho, and how even after almost 25 years, the Lebelo family did not talk much about their loss. He also related how he had struggled to take up his studies after returning from exile and yet how looking back, regardless of the hardship, this period represented the most exciting time of his life. He likened it to being at war; a time during which he felt that he was making a difference and contributing to all the changes that ultimately took place.

Another chance meeting with Gandhi Malungane and a request that he describe what happened to him on 16 June 1976, brought home to me that 'the students' referred to in the history books included young boys such as Steve and Gandhi who were only 14 years old at the time.

What also struck me was that little or nothing of what Steve and Gandhi had told me could be found in the standard historical works on the subject. One could read about the causes of the uprising, the political undercurrents and ideological implications, and eventual political ramifications of the event. But the people who actually took part in the uprising remained, in these texts, an amorphous mass or a general body of people generically referred to only as 'the students'.

Late in 2000 I approached Gandhi, Steve and a friend of Steve's, Dumisani Ntshangase, with the idea of interviewing people about 16 June 1976. We vigorously debated how we should go about this task. Who should we ask? How should we go about structuring the interviews? The 25th anniversary of the uprising was about nine months away; would it be possible to gather enough material to compile a book in time for publication in June 2001?

Wherever we found ourselves, we conducted heated discussions as to what we should do. Everyone who heard about the project was interested and offered to tell us where they had been on 16 June 1976, albeit in the remote rural areas or other cities. During lunch breaks in the concourse of the University of the Witwatersrand interested acquaintances and bystanders would hear us arguing and would offer their opinions on what form the book should take.

Our search for a more central meeting venue led us to Dumisani's favourite shebeen in Pimville, where our meetings were observed with keen interest. It took some effort to sacrifice the call of a cold beer in the quest for a structure for the book and a workable plan of action. The four people huddled together under an umbrella on the front lawn of the shebeen, working and arguing in an environment of serious relaxation, were the object of much curiosity amongst the patrons – especially since one of them was female! Even the owner of the shebeen moved closer to hear what was being discussed.

In an effort to narrow the focus of this vast topic and to make it manageable both in terms of time and financial constraints, we agreed to focus only on what happened to schoolchildren in Soweto in June 1976. Other residents of Soweto who were directly or indirectly involved in the uprising, such as teachers, parents, officials, bystanders, shop owners and paramedics, were beyond the scope of our research. What happened to the students afterwards is yet another untold story.

In finding people to interview we followed leads within our circles of friends, relatives and acquaintances. Although we recognised the danger of the lack of representivity this approach could lead to, for the means at our disposal it proved to be the most efficient and cost-effective way to proceed. As a result we spoke to people who have never been asked about what happened to them on 16 June 1976. No one who currently or at the time was in a leadership position was approached for an interview. In doing our oral interviews we tried not to 'allow the voices of interviewers to speak' (a criticism often heard in academic circles).

Instead, we tried to listen respectfully and to record accurately what we had heard.

Working on this book was an emotional experience. It evoked long-forgotten memories and emotions in the respondents, some of whom had never spoken about the events in which they had participated all those years ago. The stories evoked powerful emotions, too, in all the people who worked on the project.

Sue Krige agreed to write a section about the background to the educational system in 1976. We were privileged that Bongani Mnguni, who was a young photographer at the time and extensively covered the uprising, agreed to make available his photographs of that time, as well as to take additional photographs for the book. He was also interviewed and unwittingly provided the sub-title for the original edition of the book: 'It all started with a dog ...'

This book was not funded by any institution or grant, but was made possible by the efforts of individuals who worked after hours and over weekends. Many gaps in the narrative inevitably remain. A comprehensive, well-funded oral history research project would be needed to adequately and systematically cover what happened to a representative sample of people in all the diverse areas of Soweto as well as elsewhere on the Witwatersrand and in South Africa as a whole. Only then will a more complete picture of what happened on 16 June 1976 emerge.

Having heard the story of Abe Lebelo who died tragically on 4 August 1976 in an alley in Diepkloof close to the BP Garage on the corner of Immink Drive and the Soweto Highway, I would like to contribute in a small way to honouring the memory of a very brave young man. When he left home on that day to join the march, he knew that the police would be waiting for them, and that he would be courting danger. He had had six weeks' worth of personal experience of what the police had done and what they were capable of doing. Yet he still chose to march. He died, not accidentally as a bystander who happened to be in the line of fire, but as a young activist who believed in what he was doing and was fully aware of the consequences. He is a person I would have liked to meet.

There are many brave young men and women like Abe Lebelo whose names need to be recorded. They died, not only in Soweto in 1976, but also in other places and at other times in southern Africa. But, in as much as men, women and children who died in the Soweto uprising need to be remembered, each one of the young learners whose lives changed forever and for whom life would never be the same again, should also be remembered. They continue to carry the scars of 1976.

STEVE LEBELO

The story of 16 June 1976 is very close to my heart. The Soweto Revolt changed my life dramatically. But it also changed the lives of many who, like me, were caught up in it.

Abe, my elder brother, was killed on 4 August 1976. He was one of the most influential leaders after Tsietsi Mashinini and Khotso Seathlolo. Many believed that he was intentionally killed by the police, and so he was cast in the role of a martyr. My family was made to believe that Abe's death was not all in vain. But we were never the same again after that morning of 4 August 1976.

Until Abe was killed, I was not particularly involved with the events of 16 June 1976. Then I seemed to perceive his death as a challenge to me to pursue his goal. My mother tried to persuade me to distance myself from the struggle in 1977, urging me to write examinations in March of that year. I refused, thinking then it was an act of political commitment.

I think differently now. Years later, I realise that I could have chosen to remain uninvolved and would not be considered less of 'a man'. I often think that had I not been as involved as I was, I could have made or done other things more worthwhile than I ultimately have.

The highlight of my involvement in the book is seeing stories of lesser known people being published. I think that there are young men and women, little-known because they were not in leadership positions, whose experiences of 16 June 1976 and the consequences of their involvement were profound. I feel good that such stories are being told and are beginning to capture the imagination of people.

GANDHI MALUNGANE

For some years after 16 June 1976 I found myself confused about my participation in the event. There was criticism and condemnation from various people – politicians, academics, clerics, to name a few – of all colours. I did not know the significance of what I had taken part in or whether it was seen as good or bad. My instincts, however, kept insisting (and still do today) that my participation had been worthwhile. But I have always regretted that it gave birth to the 'necklace', the cruel style of punishing those identified as enemies of liberation.

I was born and bred in Chiawelo. When the uprising started I was a student at Nghungunyane Secondary School. I experienced the start of the uprising at Nghungunyane and witnessed many killings and burnings at various places around Chiawelo which I have never came across in any books I have read about the events.

For that reason I felt that there might be many people like myself who witnessed, experienced and participated in the uprising, but who experienced it differently to those who are mentioned in the many books about June 1976. These people almost certainly can be found in the townships forming Soweto.

I have often heard people talking about their experiences of the most essential day in the history of South Africa. Some had bad memories about the day whereas some recall good things. To some it carries a mixture of both bad and good memories. One good example is the two women in Dhlamini One and Two. To them 16 June 1976 meant a lifetime of confinement in wheelchairs. The family of a woman who was killed in Chiawelo bottle store is no exception to those who have haunting memories. And there are lots of men and women you can find in Soweto shebeens. To many of them, 16 June 1976 meant farewell to the classrooms and to their identities.

Consequently, when the opportunity arose to talk about my experiences of 16 June 1976, I thought of all those who used to think and talk about the uprising, as well as those people who might have been silent, as I had been. I felt courageous about the idea of writing a book about these missing elements. I have no doubt in my mind that with the information from these various people that has been collected and put together, South Africans now have a new glimpse of the uprising and an opportunity to discover some of the missing realities of the event.

DUMISANI NTSHANGASE

The story of 16 June 1976 is the story of South Africa. Not only has it shaped our history as a country but it has also shaped our individual thinking.

I was eleven in 1976 and doing my Standard Three (Grade Five) at Lilydale Primary School. My father was a teacher at the very same school and my mother was a teacher at another primary school in Naledi. My older brother had decided he was too old to be under parental control, so he had left home and gone to stay with my grandmother. I suppose that there was less control under granny's eye! However, some of my other siblings were in Pimville at school. Another sibling was only a year old and my youngest sister was not even born yet.

Coming from Pimville, taking a bus to Dhlamini is quite a journey for an eleven-year-old. What a journey it would prove to be on that fateful day. When the uprising broke, I was not aware of what was going on. All I knew was that things were not right. I was warned (funnily enough, not by my father who was a teacher there and should have known better) by other children at school that I would not be able to take a bus back home. Did I ever think about asking my father what I should do? I don't think so. All I know is that I walked, together with two other friends of mine, from Dhlamini to the Chiawelo station. Then we walked on the rail-tracks towards Kliptown where I would have to walk within the Pimville Golf Course until I reached home. That was safe and that is what I did.

What I now know clearly is that things were never the same again. School was not school any longer. Even my parents, teachers for that matter, encouraged me to stay home. How could they, as teachers, encourage their own child to stay home and not go to school? Now I know that things were not right.

We were not sent to boarding school or to school elsewhere. We were never arrested or shot. Yet we saw all the things that happened and even became proud of being shot by a tear-gas canister. It was the mark of heroism.

Now I am an adult, a husband and a father. I look back at those years with wonder. What actually happened? What was an ordinary day for an ordinary child? How did I manage to grow up to this?

This book is my contribution to our continuous quest to understand history from an individual's perspective. I am not interested in what 'the people' did. I am interested in what the individual did. Was it possible to play hide-and-seek and have unimaginative sexual experiments with your neighbour's seven-year-old? Was it possible to go on hunting rats and birds? Was life normal as history makes us think it was not? Who defines normality, anyway ...

SUE KRIGE

16 June made an indelible impression on me as a teacher in training and as a white woman with rather ill-formed, left-wing leanings. On that day I was teaching the fall of the Bastille to an elite class of boys at a private school. I was doing a teacher's diploma course at the University of the Witwatersrand, which included three weeks of 'teaching practice' at three different schools. Around lunch-time in the cosy staffroom, 'masters' (teachers) circulated fragments of news mixed with well-concealed anxiety. I was immediately struck by the irony of the topic I was teaching. I phoned my History lecturer, Peter Kallaway, who urged me to come back to campus to participate in a demonstration on Jan Smuts Avenue.

On the afternoon of 16 June I remember standing on Jan Smuts Avenue with hundreds of other students and a fair number of easily identifiable police spies. Students from the Rand Afrikaans University pelted us with eggs and tomatoes, and motorists swore as they went past. A number of helicopters flew overhead towards Soweto. Newspaper reports were sketchy, but full of the deaths of Hector Peterson and Dr Melville Edelstein. It was almost impossible to get an accurate idea of what was happening and why.

I have taught in many places since then, at a secondary and tertiary level. I have participated in teacher programmes on using oral tradition and testimony. I have seen the power of the spoken word in exploring history and in affirming the speaker. I have learned, I hope, to be humble in the presence of pain, joy and wisdom embedded in simple sentences. I have grasped at the things that connect us beneath the veneers of a 'cultural diversity' and a 'rainbow nation'. As a white woman, in these encounters I have made some peace with my own guilt. For me, a return to the memories of 16 June was the natural closing of a chapter which began in 1976.

Acknowledgements

We wish to acknowledge everybody who agreed to be interviewed for this project. Our sincere thanks to them all. Our appreciation of their valuable time and contribution is immense.

We would also like to thank all members of our respective families who have been understanding during the course of the research and writing of this book. Without you, it would not have been possible.

Our sincere thanks also go to:

- *Rapport* who generously allowed us to use their valuable photographs taken in June and July 1976. Outside private photographers' collections, *Rapport* seems to have the best intact photographic collection dealing with the Soweto uprising
- John Kane-Berman who graciously gave us permission to adapt and quote from his 1978 book *Soweto: Black Revolt, White Reaction*
- Caron Klass who interviewed Steve and Gandhi, and who conducted several other interviews as part of an oral history project for the final-year research component of her education diploma. She has kindly permitted us to use her research
- Gandhi Malungane who, in addition to his other duties, expended much time and effort in obtaining photographs of the respondents.
- Busi Xaba who helped to transcribe some tapes and enter data on the computer
- Agnes Mange, of 77 Sunvalley, our shebeen, who allowed us to use her space for our many meetings
- Rebecca Mosete at the City Press and Rapport Library and Kathy Brookes at MuseuMAfrica, who at very short notice efficiently assisted us with photographic research
- Themba Maseko who took additional photographs
- Wendy Job of the Department of Geography, University of the Witwatersrand, who provided a special map of Soweto
- Julie-Anne Justus, our editor, who turned the spoken word into eminently readable text without losing the tone and texture of the individual voices.
- Annari van der Merwe, our publisher, who had faith in our dream to publish this book to commemorate 16 June 1976

Select bibliography

Badat, S. (1999) *Black Student Politics: Higher Education Apartheid from SASO to SANSCO 1968 – 1990.* Pretoria: HSRC Publishers.

Bonner, P. and Segal, L. (1998) 'This is our day', in *Soweto: A History.* Cape Town: Maskew Miller Longman.

Brooks, A. and Brickhill J. (1980) *Whirlwind before the Storm.* London: IDAF.

Christie, P. (1991) *The Right to Learn: The Struggle for Education in South Africa.* Johannesburg: Ravan Press.

Diseko, N. (1991) 'The origins and development of the South Africa Student's Movement (SASM): 1968-1976', *Journal of Southern African Studies.* Vol. 18, No. 1. March.

Hirson, B. (1979) *Year of Fire, Year of Ash. The Soweto Revolt: Roots of a Revolution.* London: ZED Press.

Hyslop, J. (1999) *The Classroom Struggle: Policy and Resistance in South Africa, 1940–1990.* Pietermaritzburg: University of Natal Press.

Kane-Berman, J. (1978) *Soweto: Black Revolt, White Reaction.* Johannesburg: Ravan Press.

Klass, C. (2000) *An Oral History Account of June 16th 1976: The Soweto uprising within the Context of Education.* Unpublished Independent Study: Department of Educational Studies, Johannesburg College of Education.

Lodge, T. (1983) 'Children of Soweto', in *Black Politics in South Africa since 1945.* Johannesburg: Ravan Press.

Magubane, P. (1986) *June 16: Fruit of Fear.* Johannesburg: Skotaville.

Mamdoo, F. (1998) 'What happened to Mabuyisa?' Emdomol Productions.

Ndlovu, S. (1998) *The Soweto uprisings: Counter-Memories of June 16.* Randburg: Ravan Press.

NECC (1987) *What is History? A New Approach to History for Students, Workers and Communities.* Johannesburg: Skotaville Press.

New Nation, New History (1989) Johannesburg: The History Workshop and New Nation.

Nuttall, T. et al. (1998) *From Apartheid to Democracy: South Africa 1948-1994.* Pietermaritzburg: Shuter and Shooter.

Pape, J. et al. (1998) *Making History Grade 12.* Sandton: Heinemann.

Seekings, J. (1993) *Heroes or Villains? Youth Politics in the 1980s.* Johannesburg: Ravan Press.